THE
MASTERY
OF
LIFE

THE MASTERY OF LIFE

A TOLTEC GUIDE TO
PERSONAL FREEDOM

DON MIGUEL RUIZ JR.

Hier⊕phant publishing

Cover design by Emma Smith
Cover art by Ričardas Anusauskas &
suns07butterfly || Shutterstock
Map of Teotihuacan by Frame25 Productions
Quetzalcoatl Illustration by Abdullah Al Mahmud Masum
Print book interior design by Frame25 Productions

Hierophant Publishing
San Antonio, TX
www.hierophantpublishing.com

If you are unable to order this book from your local bookseller,
you may order directly from the publisher.

Library of Congress Control Number: 2021943375
ISBN 978-1-950253-08-1
10 9 8 7 6 5 4 3 2 1

To all whom I love.

Contents

Explanation of Key Terms

xiii

Introduction: The Toltec Path

xv

1. The Art of Life

1

2. The Plaza of Quetzalcoatl

25

3. The Island of Safety

43

4. The Plaza of the Mind

59

5. The Plaza of Water

85

6. The Plaza of Air
111

7. The Plaza of Fire
129

8. The Plaza of Earth
151

9. The Pyramid of the Moon
173

10. The Pyramid of the Sun
191

Conclusion: Journey's End
205

Acknowledgments
209

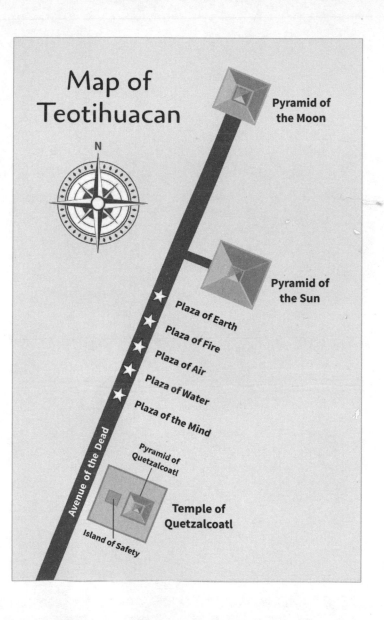

Map of Teotihuacan

N

Pyramid of
the Moon

Pyramid of
the Sun

Plaza of Earth

Plaza of Fire

Plaza of Air

Plaza of Water

Plaza of the Mind

Avenue of the Dead

Pyramid of
Quetzalcoatl

Temple of
Quetzalcoatl

Island of Safety

An artistic rendering of Quetzalcoatl, the legendary feathered serpent of Mesoamerica for which the Temple and Pyramid of Quetzalcoatl at Teotihuacan are named.

Explanation of Key Terms

Agreements: The process by which the ideas in our minds become beliefs, and consequently influence our actions.

Awareness: The practice of paying attention in the present moment to what is happening inside your body and your mind as well as in your immediate surroundings.

Domestication: The primary system of control in the Dream of the Planet. Starting when we are very young, we are presented with either a reward or a punishment for adopting the beliefs and behaviors others find acceptable. When we do this as a result of either reward or punishment, we become domesticated.

Dream of the Planet: The combination of the personal dreams of every being in the world—or the world we live in.

Mitote: The negative voices in our minds that speak to us throughout the day. Often, these voices were planted in us during our formative years, as a result of domestication.

Nagual: The Divine inside of you; the force that gives life to your mind and your body. It's similar to the concept of the spirit or the soul found in many religious traditions, but it's not exactly the same.

Personal dream: The unique reality created by every individual; your personal perspective. It is the manifestation of the relationship between your mind and your body.

Toltec people: An ancient group of Native Americans who came together in south and central Mexico to study perception. The word *Toltec* means "artist."

Toltec Warrior: One who is committed to using the teachings of the Toltec tradition to win the inner battle against domestication and attachment.

Introduction

The Toltec Path

Words are powerful tools.

In the Toltec tradition to which I belong, we say that words are the brushes we use to paint the masterpieces of our lives. Words can shift perspectives, create clarity, and reveal opportunities; conversely, they can also be used to spread anger, fear, or hate. Thus the words we choose can either lift us up or tear us down.

Words are also the primary tools we use to communicate with one another and build almost everything in our existence. Seen in this light, it's no wonder that the opening line of the Christian Gospel of John is: "In the beginning was the Word."

Our words occur first as thoughts in our minds, then as symbols with meanings that allow us to communicate and think in intellectual ways—constructing arguments, building complex stories, and, of course, *making agreements*. The human mind is brilliant at making agreements.

In the Toltec tradition, agreements are the result of the process by which the ideas in our minds become beliefs, and consequently influence our actions. These agreements can follow us throughout our entire lives, coloring our perceptions in every aspect of our day-to-day living. Our agreements, concerning everything from major decisions like whom we marry to seemingly trivial choices like what to wear, can work to inform, influence, and sometimes even control us—often without any conscious awareness on our part.

Most of our agreements run deep; they are created and cemented into "reality" by our wordy, thinking minds. We forget that thoughts and ideas, which are the building blocks of our agreements and thus our beliefs, don't exist "out there in the world." *They only exist inside us.* And they only have power because we believe they are true. The more attached we are to a particular agreement, the more power it has over us.

Agreements themselves are neither inherently positive or negative, and we rely on many of them to navigate our way through the world successfully. The agreements we entered into as children in response to our parents' instructions on safety and good health are useful:

Vegetables are nutritious and healthy. Look both ways before you cross the street. Some agreements may not be constructive or positive, however: *My contributions at work aren't worth much. I'm just not a creative person.* And some may even be self-destructive: *I am not worthy of being loved.*

Many of our agreements are the result of intellectual seeds planted inside us by others in our formative years. Learning how to recognize these agreements, discerning whether they are helpful or unhelpful, and then changing or dismissing them if necessary make up one of the major endeavors of those on a journey to personal freedom.

So while words can be very powerful, in the Toltec tradition we also recognize that words are extremely limited. They are only descriptors and indicators of reality, not reality itself. As philospher Alan Watts notes in regards to words: "The menu is not the meal." Words can only point to the truth; they are not the truth in and of themselves.

Books are amazing tools which, after all, are made up of words. The right book at the right time has the power to transform lives by offering hope in times of despair or provoking wonder in times of creative drought. But for all that books are incredible pockets of potential, it is ultimately not the book itself that changes us. *We change ourselves.*

This presents us with an interesting challenge here. To explain the teachings and tools I will share with you here, I need to use words. But I invite you to allow these words to go beyond your mind and into your heart. It's only then—in what I call the synchronicity of heart and mind—that transformation can occur.

Beyond Mind

The ancient Greeks had a word for this. They called it *metanoia*—literally, "beyond mind." Metanoia can be understood as a transformation of the individual that occurs simultaneously in both the mind and the heart. This is the spirit in which I would like the words of this book to be taken. I hope that they prompt you to turn inward, to move beyond logic and reason into a place of luminous openness and fresh awareness. There is a sense of movement here—of turning around, of going beyond, of opening up. And that is because, ultimately, whether we realize it or not, we are all on one long magnificent journey—the journey to personal freedom and the liberation of our true selves. The goal of this journey is a fundamental change in our perception of the world and our place in it.

Perception is, in fact, what the ancient Toltecs came together to study and understand over 2,000 years ago. According to the oral tradition of my family, the ancients knew that the greatest freedom lies in the art of seeing reality as it truly is, beyond our agreements and stories. What they found is that no real change is possible without clear perception.

And what is the greatest obstacle to clear perception? Fear.

Fear is at the heart of every obstacle we encounter on our way to personal freedom. It is important to note, however, that when I use the word *fear* in this context, I am referring to psychological fear rather than physical fear. Physical fear can be natural and helpful, for instance, if you suddenly encounter a bear while hiking in the woods. Fear in this case produces adrenaline, which elevates your heart rate and increases your oxygen intake. It prepares your body to either stand and fight or run for your life.

Contrast this with psychological fear—the fear that others won't like you, that you won't get what you want, or that you're not "good enough." These types of fear are all based on the agreements you have made throughout your life. Sadly, this psychological fear often produces the same physical reactions in our bodies that physical fear does, sending us into the same heart-pounding, gut-wrenching response. This puts our bodies through an inordinate amount of unnecessary physical stress that, over the course of a lifetime, can have harmful consequences.

Why do I say that fear is the greatest obstacle to clear perception when there are so many other negative emotions to consider? Because, in most cases, fear sits at the center of all of these other emotions. The vast majority of the time, anger, hate, jealousy, regret, and virtually all other negative reactions can ultimately be traced back to fear. Fear paralyzes us into thinking that we will repeat the mistakes of the past and overwhelms us with anxieties about the future. Fear keeps us trapped in the false belief that we are only acceptable when we live up to an unending list of expectations—we must be smart enough, pretty enough, spiritual enough, financially stable enough, accomplished enough, etc. When we work with and learn how to recognize and deal with our fears, we often find that the other negative emotions we struggle with diminish or even evaporate at the same time.

Much of the journey we will share in these pages will tackle this issue of fear, since overcoming its psychological manifestations is such a huge and important step on the road to clear perception and personal freedom.

The Journey

In the Toltec tradition, the journey to clear perception can include an actual physical journey that takes its inspiration from the spiritual center of my Toltec ancestors, the ancient pyramid complex found at the city of Teoti-huacan (sometimes shortened to "Teo" in these pages). This ancient complex is located about twenty-five miles outside modern-day Mexico City. The buildings, temples, roadways, and pyramids of Teo provide the map we will follow to do the work described in this book.

Each of the locations within the pyramid complex has special meaning and significance that can be seen as symbolic of a stage on the path to personal freedom. I have traveled through the complex myself many times over the course of thirty years, initially as a student of my father and grandmother, and later as a teacher. The majesty of the city's architectural achievements alone is a testament to the wisdom of the ancient people who built it.

But while I encourage you to visit this remarkable place if you are ever able to do so, I also want to be clear that you do not need to travel to Teotihuacan to benefit from the work described here. That's because the most important journey you can ever make is the one within yourself. All the examination, preparation, and work you need to do is inside you. All the wisdom you need to live a life of personal mastery lies inside your heart and your mind right now. The teachings of Teo, and those I present in this book, act merely to help you uncover and open to the power you already possess.

In the Toltec tradition, we teach that, while all the wisdom and answers you need are within you, sometimes we all need a guide to help us find them. And that is the goal of this book. In it, I give a variety of exercises and rituals designed to help you perform this inner work. Ritual and ceremony hold an important place in the Toltec tradition—but not because we have any particular attachment to religious practices or because we are led by superstitions. In fact, we reject both of these. Instead, we perform rituals and ceremonies because they have the power to reach parts of our being beyond the mind.

Rituals rely on sensory experience and our relationship to time and space. In them, we start in one place and end in another, and we find that we have been changed. Rituals open up space in our bodies, minds, and hearts. I encourage you to throw yourself wholeheartedly into the exercises, rituals, and ceremonies at the end of the chapters of this book. Our minds often dismiss the power of rituals and ceremonies precisely because their efficacy transcends our intellectual capacity. That's okay. Think of the mind in this instance as being like grumpy teenagers who don't want you to dance at the party because you might embarrass them. They'll live. Do it anyway. Sometimes the best way to overcome the mind is simply to ignore it.

Mastery

It is important to say something here about the title of this book. Let me be clear about what I mean by *mastery*. In the modern world, *to master* something can sometimes mean to exert ultimate will or control over it—for instance, to give orders to someone, or to be in a position of power, or to win, or to dominate people, places, or situations.

You won't find any of that in this book.

Mastery, in the context of this book, refers to that which we practice regularly. In these pages, I ask you to take a deep look at what you believe about yourself and the world around you, and to notice what you habitually do—how you act and react based on what you believe. Then, once you have become more aware of what you think, how you act, and where those thoughts and actions originate, I invite you to practice *new* ways of thinking, acting, and being that are more aligned with your true nature and your highest good. I encourage you to practice a life uncontrolled by fear.

The title of this book is not meant to imply that it will somehow empower you to control life or force your will onto other people, places, or things. In fact, when you become a true master, you release the need for any of this. Instead, you strive to align your individual will with that of life itself, doing your best in all situations, letting go of categories and separations, and surrendering to the outcome. You come to understand that life knows better than you do. This understanding brings you a peace that goes deeper and lasts longer than any short-term gain you might enjoy by exerting control or power.

Another way to say all of this is: *When you master life, you see God everywhere you look.* Of course, this is easy to do when viewing a beautiful sunset over a mountain but much more difficult when faced with the carnage of war. Yet, regardless of how you feel about the sunset or the carnage, life moves through both in equal measure.

Because of this, the journey in this book is about learning how to surrender to life rather than having some type of egoic domination over it. The beautiful paradox is that it's through this spirit of surrender that we actually do gain a measure of control—over ourselves, over our actions and reactions, and over the choices we make. And this can lead us to a new place of peace, happiness, and personal freedom. This is the gift my Toltec ancestors offered to the world centuries ago, and it is my privilege to offer it to you now.

So let us take a deep breath together and prepare to step onto the path. We are standing at the beginning of an amazing journey.

Chapter 1

The Art of Life

Imagine the moment of your birth.

Breathing, moving, and feeling your way through this new environment, you entered the world as a being of pure awareness, spirit, emotions, and instincts. And this miracle of life, the amazing bundle of capacities that is you, arrived here possessed of extraordinary potential—the potential to build a life of joy, wonder, freedom, and creativity. Even more remarkably, while all human beings have these capacities, each of us is also a unique individual with the opportunity to become a fully realized, creative, loving person. Thus we are all artists, and our lives are our art. In fact, the very word *Toltec* means "artist." The ancient Toltecs believed that the idea of art went far beyond the scope of what we may consider art today. And they mastered the great art of life and spiritual freedom by learning how to recognize and tap into the radiant energy and potential that move through all things.

In the Toltec tradition, we believe that this pure life-force—this energy and potential—is present in each and every one of us. We call this energy the *nagual*. Countless other cultures and spiritual traditions have recognized and honored this vital life force as well, and it's known by many names: *chi, shakti, prana, the Holy Spirit, baraka, wakan,* etc. This essential, animating energy is always around us. It moves through every living thing and is shaped by our intention. The nagual has been present in you and all those around you from the moment you came into the world.

Domestication

Immediately upon your birth—if not before, given the tools of modern technology—you were given a name and assigned a sex. At that moment, the beginnings of what it means to be "you" were formed. Those who welcomed you into this world took care of your basic needs, providing food, shelter, and love in the best way they knew how. But they also had the job of helping you learn how to live among others within a specific set of collective cultural beliefs.

So in addition to the basic care they provided, your parents or caregivers also "hooked" your attention. Over the next few years, they taught you your name; they told you a story about your birth and your family; they identified you as either a girl or a boy. And they taught you what all of that meant in the society in which you lived. As you grew older, they directed you toward a pattern of likes and dislikes, and taught you about social and cultural norms: *In this family, we do/don't dance or sing. In our culture, men don't cry.* You probably accepted many of these ideas and rebelled against others. But in either case, the stories, norms, and preferences began to form your identity, or the image you have of yourself.

Likewise, your parents or caretakers shared with you their ideas, opinions, judgments, goals, and desires. And they also shared their fears, some of which were doubtless expressed in order to keep you safe: *Don't touch the stove. Watch for cars before crossing the street.* Directives like these were helpful and necessary. But there were, of course, many other fears they shared with you indirectly—fear of not being liked, fear of not having enough, or fear of not *being* enough. These fears also play a protective role, of course, as the human animal is social and communal. In certain circumstances, not fitting in can be quite dangerous, or even deadly.

This process of slow acculturation, in which we are taught, directly or indirectly, a body of beliefs, fears, preferences, and habits, is one the Toltec tradition calls *domestication*. As you become domesticated, you acquire the beliefs and behaviors that you grow to think of as your "self." In short, you form an identity of what it means to be you. This may sound negative or pessimistic, but it is not. It is simply an unavoidable process that we all go through as human beings.

The fact that domestication is unavoidable, however, doesn't mean that it doesn't have negative consequences. As you grow up and become domesticated, your original birthright—the essential light in you that aligns with the nagual—often gets buried under a confusing heap of emotions, rules, and agreements that guide your every move and serve to separate you from your deepest truth.

But what if you could uncover this truth?

All over the world and throughout time, mystics and seekers have walked a path dedicated to uncovering their own truth and personal freedom. These spiritual travelers do not hope to return to their infant state, but instead to move beyond their current way of being to something much richer. By reclaiming their personal power, they rekindle the pure awareness that was theirs at birth and aspire to a new, mature ability to transform their personal experience in ways that enable them to create, to play, to love, and to find joy in the challenges of life.

They embrace unconditional love as the perfect mirror of everything they see, and they stand strong in the face of every internal and external force that seeks to destroy their inner peace. They no longer let fear control them. This is personal freedom. This is the Toltec path. This is the mastery of life.

The Ancient City of Teotihuacan

Long before the Aztecs came to south-central Mexico, the region was home to the Toltec people, who lived and prospered there. The greatest architectural achievement of this ancient people is the pyramid complex at Teotihuacan, a structure that was abandoned by its inhabitants 500 years before the Aztecs arrived. No known written language and very few facts about the people who lived there have survived. In fact, we know little to nothing of their government, their social structures, their religion, or their history.

The sophisticated architecture and art that the Aztecs found at this complex impressed them so much that they decided it must have been the birthplace of the gods themselves. They named it *Teotihuacan*, which means "the place where man becomes God"; however, a better translation for the modern world might be "the place where humans recognize the divinity within themselves."

Today, we know that, by 500 CE, at the height of its development, the city supported a population of around 200,000 people, making it one of the largest cities in the world at that time. Although archaeologists and anthropologists may disagree about the facts of Toltec life and culture, my family and many others have long preserved a rich oral tradition filled with myths, stories, and teachings that illuminate the Toltec path. The goal of this path has always been the same—to find personal freedom through transforming our fear-based outlook into one of unconditional love and happiness.

The impressive remains of the city of Teotihuacan are revered today as a place of great spiritual power. Seekers travel from all over the world to continue their own quest for personal freedom by completing a power journey through the city. They walk the Avenue of the Dead, moving between the great pyramids of Quetzalcoatl, the Moon, and the Sun, which are ingeniously oriented to the cardinal directions, the night sky, and the seasons.

My family draws on generational wisdom about the complex itself, tying the inward spiritual journey that each of us makes in this life to the outward aspects of the ancient city. In other words, each of the avenues, plazas, and temples corresponds to a stage on the inner path. And this is the path we will follow through this book.

Each chapter corresponds to a different place in the complex, and each stage on the journey illuminates and deepens our understanding of the path to self-realization and personal freedom.

Essential within this tradition is the understanding that these teachings are both ancient and modern, and they are always evolving. Toltecs have described this path for many generations and have taught others to walk along it. Yet here is the paradox: This path is, and can only be, unique for each individual. As my grandmother always told us: "If you practice the Toltec tradition the way your father or I practice it, then you are killing the tradition." It took me some time to understand what she meant, and that was that the tradition will always be unique to the person practicing it because it will be based on their individual experiences after applying the lessons in their life.

Personal and Collective Dreams

The Toltec tradition teaches that the mind is dreaming all the time. From the moment you wake up, until the moment you fall asleep, your mind is actively perceiving, creating stories, and trying to make sense of what it perceives. This is what the Toltecs refer to as the *personal dream*. This reminds us that our understanding of the world is filtered through our own perceptions, domestications, and experiences. This is part of the reason why the Toltecs do not have specific rules or doctrines that apply to everyone. While the journey of healing—the path of the Toltec Warrior—has been walked by many before you, there is only one person who can walk it in your life: *You*.

Because we do not journey through our lives alone, there is also a *collective* dream, which the Toltec tradition refers to as the *Dream of the Planet*. This is defined as the sum total of all personal dreams, and we say it is our collective dream that has created the world as we know it. In this book, I will go one step further and introduce the *Dream of the Universe*, which encompasses all the scientific and technical knowledge we have acquired of stars, planets, and galaxies far beyond our own. The Dream of the Universe makes room for our ever-expanding perception in this new frontier.

The consistent theme underpinning all of these ways of knowing and being—personal dreams, the Dream of the Planet, and the Dream of the Universe—is the Toltec Warrior's understanding that *it is our perception that creates our reality*. In the Toltec tradition, this is not a metaphor; we mean it quite literally.

The Warrior's Path

One of the remarkable things about the ancient Toltecs is that they were focused on self-realization and awareness, not on war and domination over others. The Toltec Warrior is thus not a warrior in the sense of someone who is trained to kill, to defend, or to conquer in any military sense. Toltec Warriors focus on the spiritual war being waged within themselves. Their ultimate goal is to live from a place of universal love and acceptance rather than fear, greed, and hate.

The image of the warrior reminds us that this path holds the promise of great reward. It is accessible to all, but it is not easy. The warrior's path begins with the realization that we must go inward first, as no progress can be made without reflection on our innermost world: the mind itself. We must come to understand how the mind works. After all, we can't understand anything, feel anything, believe anything, or make any spiritual progress without using our minds.

Although we start off as infants—little bundles of pure light and energy closely aligned with the nagual source—we soon learn to use our minds. Through the process of domestication, however, our perception becomes corrupted with unhelpful beliefs and agreements. Although we all want to live a life that can be described as a beautiful dream, both our personal and collective dreams can become corrupted to the point that they feel more like nightmares instead. The most obvious result of this is seen in war and the violence we inflict on one another. But the origin of all this outer suffering can always be traced back to the conflict within ourselves.

Fundamental to all outer conflict is the inner idea that we don't have enough of what we think we need, or that we are not enough as we are. Anytime we judge ourselves as not having enough or not being enough (skilled enough, smart enough, tough enough, etc.), we cause ourselves and others suffering. Sadly, many of us today spend more waking hours in mental suffering than in peace, so it's no surprise that some are living in a nightmare instead of a beautiful dream. One of the things we learn on the warrior's path is to recognize where and when we cause our own suffering and how this suffering is based only on our perception.

In his book *The Wisdom of the Shamans* (Hierophant Publishing, 2018), my brother don José explains that, in the current Dream of the Planet, the human mind has what could be called a habit of, or even an addiction to, suffering. While that may seem an odd assertion at first, if you look at all the ways humans cause suffering to each other and themselves, I believe you'll find that it's true.

Starting with all the little ways we cause emotional harm to one another through habits like gossip and right up to and beyond the horrific destruction of war, we ourselves are by far the main source of human suffering. Even when we look inside ourselves, we can see our own tendencies to gravitate toward suffering. For instance, have you ever noticed how we often look for problems when things get too peaceful? And how about our collective love of drama? Turn on any television and you won't have to wait very long to see an example of this.

The root of all of this mental suffering is psychological fear—either the fear that we won't get something we want (a material object, recognition or praise, the love of others) or the fear that we will lose something we already have. The irony is that most of our fears are based on domesticated ideas rather than our internal truth.

For example, many of us today take on jobs and acquire possessions or status simply because others do. We convince ourselves that we "should do" or "should have" them as well. We live in a world of comparisons, and we tie our own self-worth and self-acceptance to metrics created by others rather than to an honest investigation of our own wants and needs. Some have been living this way for so long that they have become unaware of what they really want for themselves. As you can imagine—or may even have experienced—this behavior inevitably leads to suffering rather than happiness.

The goal of Toltec Warriors is to recognize and break free from fear-based agreements and unhelpful beliefs and fully realize themselves as spiritual beings alive *right now*—as perfect and whole manifestations of the nagual, or life itself. In this way, they become the artists whose creations are the stories of their own lives. In these new dreams of their own making, they take actions that are consistent with what they really want in life.

To this aim, taking a power journey can be a helpful tool on the path.

Power Journeys

At its most basic level, a power journey is a ceremonial trip taken to and within a sacred place. This is often a ruin, a monument, or a natural site that has been used across time and tradition to gather spiritual power, celebrate rituals, and hold ceremonies that advance individual and collective transformation and freedom. Places like these exist all over the world, of course, from medicine wheels in the American West, to Table Mountain in South Africa, to Stonehenge in the English countryside or the Camino de Santiago in Spain. My family has long traveled to Teotihuacan on power journeys, often introducing apprentices and other seekers to the sacred path we walk there. This path takes us from the Plaza of Quetzalcoatl to the Pyramid of the Sun, moving through the ancient ruins in a ceremonial way.

At the end of a power journey to a sacred place, people often find that they have profoundly shifted their own perspective. They see things differently—with an enhanced sensory experience that lasts long after they return to their "normal" lives. They may also soak in the energy and wisdom of past travelers. We feel their supportive presence as the architects of these sacred spaces and as guides who transcend the limits of time to reach our hearts and minds through their creations. In many native traditions, these places also tend to be deeply rooted in the power of the natural world and the four primordial elements (water, air, fire, earth). Because of this, a power journey can leave us with a renewed connection to the earth itself, as well as to the sun and moon, to plant and animal life, and to the vastness of our universe.

A power journey may be tied to a physical place, but it does not have to be. In the Toltec tradition, we say that any outward journey is a lesser journey; the greater journey is the one you take within yourself.

Most outward journeys, including the path we follow at Teo, are linear. We move from one point to another along a predetermined course. By contrast, inner journeys are more akin to a never-ending spiral. As you walk the path of the Toltec Warrior, you will see that there are circumstances and situations in your life that you will return to again and again, each time with heightened awareness. If you don't learn what the situation has to teach you, the lesson will be repeated. The work is never done; mastery is always a journey in progress. It should thus be no surprise that the symbol of the spiral has been found as part of ancient petroglyphs all over the world.

Although the path has no end, this doesn't mean that warriors don't have goals toward which they work. Their goal throughout this journey is to move beyond any fear-based domesticated agreements they are holding so they can begin to live the life of the artist—one based in joy and unconditional love.

Did the ancient people who built Teo ever envision us walking this path today? We will never know. But I feel certain that they were just as aware, if not more so, of the importance of this journey toward the mastery of life as we are today.

Fear and Love

This not a journey for the faint of heart. It asks you to examine your identity, your desires, and your domestications, and requires that you give up the "little self" that occupies so much of your everyday life. Your domestications are deeply ingrained. And because we become so attached to these parts of ourselves—so much so that we often think of them as the sum total of who we are—this process can create the exact psychological fear that you are working to eliminate.

There are a couple of reasons for this. First, when you give up the safety of the known, even if what's known is painful, you almost always feel fear. For instance, how many times have you chosen to stay in a bad situation, perhaps a job or a relationship, because it was familiar and comfortable? Second—and this may come as a surprise to you—deep down, many of us are afraid of our own true potential, afraid of aligning with the unique light that we are and letting it shine brightly in the world. Perhaps you wonder whether stepping into your personal power will alienate or offend the people around you and the groups to which you belong. And what if you can never go back to the comforts of being meek and unaware?

These are common fears. But they are purely psychological in nature. Moreover, these fears are illusory. What lies just beyond them is a beautiful way of being in the world, one where fear is replaced by unconditional love. This doesn't mean that you won't experience the human emotion of fear from time to time. Rather, it means that fear will no longer control your life. It means that, when fear occurs, you can recognize and transform it.

Psychological fears dominate modern life, wreaking havoc on our bodies and minds, and feeding a nonstop addiction to self-judgment, guilt, and suffering. The prevalence of this type of fear is perhaps the biggest single indicator of someone whose personal dream has become a nightmare.

When fear is your main motivation, your behaviors, relationships, and emotions are hijacked by a powerful inner voice that claims to be protecting you, but is really causing havoc. Fear leads you to keep your true self hidden behind masks and personality traits. It undermines your deepest desires and causes you to build walls or push away the love of others. Fear also encourages you to try to control current situations and predict the future, even though the only moment ever accessible to you is the present one. Finally, fear tells you the biggest lie of all—that you are small and insignificant, and that you are somehow separate from all of creation.

The goal of the warrior's path is to replace this fear with love. But in the Toltec tradition, we recognize that there are two manifestations of love: conditional and unconditional.

Conditional love functions only to obscure your deeper reality through domestication. At the root of all domestication, there is inevitably some kind of condition. *If I do this, then I will be worthy of love.* Manifestations of this also appear to others. *If you do or say the right things (get the right grades or job), then I will give you my approval and love.* The corollary and inherent threat, of course, is that, if you fail to do these things, love will be withheld from you. The key to conditional love is the if/then statement. But there is no place for if/then statements in unconditional love.

By contrast, *unconditional love* flows directly from the nagual through our hearts and out into the world as we engage with other human beings and all life through the lens of compassion. Unconditional love recognizes that the nagual—the divine nature and the energy of life itself—flows through all living beings and is therefore present in every person you meet, regardless of who they are or whether you agree with them on matters of culture, religion, politics, or any other way of being or thinking. The achievement of true mastery is reflected in your ability to see this reality clearly in all living beings. *There is only love.*

That is why this is a warrior's path. You do, after all, have true power that flows from the nagual inside you, though it may be clouded over by all sorts of agreements, judgments, and fears. Regardless, your power never resides in those places where fear keeps you cowering—your possessions, your status, your intellect, or any of the personalities or masks you may wear on different occasions. The true source of your power, your birthright, is your union with life itself—which is always there, whether or not you have lost sight of it or buried it.

This journey has to start at the only place it can—where you are *right now*. Step into this moment and radically accept where you are right now as being the absolute perfect place you are meant to be. Everything that has happened up until this moment has made you who you are and brought you here. Nothing in your life has been a mistake.

Preparing for the Journey

At the start of any journey, you pack the things you want to take with you. Likewise, for this inner journey, I suggest you acquire two specific tools that I will reference throughout the book—a journal and a place for meditation.

EXERCISE: JOURNALING

For your journal, choose a blank notebook of some kind that resonates with you. It doesn't have to be fancy, but it should attract you enough so that you are drawn to keep it nearby and use it. Many people choose a journal by the feel of it— that is, it has a certain energy and potential in its physical presence. Your journal will be a place to write down many aspects of your journey, and it can be a powerful way to remember and reinforce what you learn and discover as you make your way.

If the idea of writing in a physical journal by hand doesn't appeal to you, you can, of course, keep a journal on your laptop or other device. For some, typing is a faster medium that helps to create a sense of flow conducive to free association and expression. Do what works best for you.

You may wish to make a ritual out of your journaling by setting aside a fixed amount of time and/or lighting a candle to make your writing a sacred act. This isn't necessary, however, if it doesn't resonate with you.

For now, in the early stages of your journey, try using one of these questions to get started:

- At the end of the journey of my life, what would I like to feel?

- What are my greatest fears about taking this trip?

- What am I willing to accept (about myself or the power journey I am undertaking) in this moment, even if I don't like it?

EXERCISE: SITTING MEDITATION

Meditation can be a powerful tool for learning more about yourself. Of course, some of you reading this may have tried meditation in the past and found it frustrating because you could not "quiet your mind." This isn't necessarily the primary goal of meditation, however, and it's not our aim here. I want you to practice sitting meditation, not to clear your mind, but simply to watch it work. In addition, I know that the word *meditation* may be intimidating for some, but keep in mind that all you are doing is sitting quietly, nothing more. Words are only your agreements, so if the word *meditation* bothers you, choose another one—like *sitting*, or *prayer*, or *silence*.

You don't need to set up an elaborate space for meditation; all you need is a quiet place where you can be undisturbed for ten to twenty minutes. Some people like to sit on the floor in one of the classic meditation postures, but this isn't required. The best beginning posture for most is to sit in a chair with your back straight, your feet flat on the floor, and your hands resting lightly on the tops of your thighs. Most find that they can focus better with their eyes closed. Some prefer to repeat a word or phrase. For our purposes, one of the most basic and easily accessible methods of focus is simply to watch your breath. Notice it come in, and notice it go out. This is really all there is to meditation.

Once you've settled into your meditation posture and started to follow your breath, you may start to experience thoughts, emotions, and daydreams as they move through your mind. Don't try to change them or stop them; just watch them move through and then let them go. If you find yourself caught up in any given thought, emotion, or daydream (which is easy to do), simply return to your breath and commit to just observing. Over time, you may find that this becomes easier and that, while you didn't set out to quiet your mind, it just happens naturally. You will find various meditations throughout this book.

EXERCISE: SELF-ACCEPTANCE MEDITATION

In addition to packing for your journey, I suggest a little unpacking as well. As much as possible, try letting go of expectations of the future, or thoughts of how you have "failed" in the past. Here, at the very beginning of your journey, you can begin by accepting yourself just as you are, right now.

This short meditation will signal the beginning of our journey together. Feel free to take as long as you need for this, but five to ten minutes should be sufficient. The goal here is to sink into this moment and accept yourself as you are. There's no need to find the "perfect" spot for this meditation. Wherever you are reading these words in this moment will do. Simply relax and take three deep, cleansing breaths. Imagine pure energy and a golden light flowing through you and all around you.

Now say to yourself (out loud or quietly to yourself): "I accept myself exactly as I am in this moment."

If you find there are any recurring thoughts coming to you from the past, imagine the threads tying you to the past being gently cut. Allow any regrets or preoccupying memories to float out and away from you. Likewise, if you find there are anxieties and worries bothering you about the future, imagine the threads tying you to the future being gently cut, and allow these anxieties to float away from you like balloons.

Now return to this mantra: I accept myself exactly as I am in this moment. Breathe in, breathe out. Repeat the mantra. Put this book down and continue with this practice for the next few minutes. Rest in the peace of the nagual within.

Chapter 2

The Plaza of Quetzalcoatl

Imagine you find yourself standing on a stage in the middle of a large auditorium filled with hundreds of people. You aren't sure how you got there or what you are supposed to do. But as you look around, you realize that you're the only one onstage and that everyone in the audience is looking at you.

They all seem to be waiting for you to do something, but you aren't sure what that is. As you look into the faces of those in attendance, you realize that some are smiling, while others have stern or even angry looks, and still others look bored or apathetic.

Suddenly, those who are smiling start to encourage you to dance, sing, and act as music begins to play and a microphone lowers from the ceiling. Those who look stern or angry begin to yell that they don't like that music, they want another selection and maybe a new singer. Those who look bored begin to choose sides with the others. Some tell you that you're no good at any of this and you should get off the stage. Others applaud your efforts and tell you that you're the best. Many critique your appearance. One comments that you are a sloppy dresser; another claims you are cute. Everyone in the audience begins offering all sorts of advice as to what you should do next.

Before long, most are arguing among themselves while shouting directives at you. The noise of their shouts combined with the music becomes deafening. Everyone has an opinion of what you should do, and they are all vying for your attention.

Some of these opinions you agree with, and some you don't. While some of the voices are helpful, many are not. You try to listen only to the voices you like, but then you look down at your own body and notice that you barely recognize yourself. You are like a hyperactive chameleon, changing shape, size, and color in accordance with all the different opinions and advice swirling around you. Terrified, you run off the stage, find a bathroom, and lock yourself in. Staring at your own reflection in the mirror above the sink, you settle down. You can see yourself. You begin to remember who you really are.

This experience sounds like a nightmare for which very few of us would volunteer. But, in a way, we have already been living a version of this scenario all our lives. Toltecs call this the *mitote*, the voices in your mind that bombard you with all kinds of conflicting messages and clamor for your attention. These are the voices that have domesticated you. One of the simplest and most obvious forms of the mitote occurs in commercial advertising, which constantly inundates us with the idea that if we just have this product or that service, we will somehow be attractive or successful or powerful or good enough, and that our lives will then be happy. Of course, these messages are only put out there because they work so well, which shows us that they are often the result of the conditioning we received in the early years of our domestication.

Without awareness, we can live our whole lives surrounded by this chaotic babble, basing our actions and feelings on the opinions, ideas, and beliefs of others, rather than finding out who we really are and what we really want for ourselves. Unfortunately for some, this type of tap dancing to the beat of others' tunes can go on well after their formative years. Eventually, attempting to live up to the expectations of others can become so natural that they don't even notice that they're doing it. They think it's just how life is supposed to be.

In the physical power journey we undertake at Teo, we explore the mitote at our first stop, in a place that is appropriately called the Sea of Hell. This is the beginning of your path to awakening from fear and stepping into love and acceptance.

The Sea of Hell

The Sea of Hell is located in the Plaza of Quetzalcoatl, a large, open area in front of the Pyramid of Quetzalcoatl at the southern end of the Avenue of the Dead. On our physical power journeys at Teo, we walk along the length of this avenue over several days of rituals and ceremonies before we arrive at our final destination, the Pyramid of the Sun.

The center of this plaza is called the Sea of Hell because it represents the Dream of the Planet as we know it right now, constructed by all the little egos inside each of us, all clamoring for the control and attention of others. The egos of those who came before us have made all sorts of rules, judgments, and agreements that, together, add up to what we call our culture, or reality itself. Of course, we then join them and follow the edicts of society almost unconsciously. Before long, we are trying to control and manipulate ourselves and others because we fear what will happen if we don't follow these rules. When we do so, we become blind to the truth of who and what we are.

When our parents or caretakers started this process, it was almost always with good intentions. From the very beginning, the adults who loved us and cared for us set about sharing with us the knowledge they thought we needed in order to survive. They wanted to teach us certain rules and beliefs so that we would fit in. They wanted to domesticate us so that we could join the human family and survive and thrive within it.

The problems start when domestication becomes muddled with the emotional wounds of others. For example, one common and necessary act of domestication involves teaching children about the physical danger of fire. After all, children need to know about what is safe and what is not. We would be putting our children in grave danger if we didn't teach them that fire can burn, suffocate, and destroy. So we teach fire safety from a very young age, and that's good.

But then there is that other layer of domestication that relates to *psychological* rather than physical danger. In the case of fire, let's say that when you were a young child, your mother came into the garage and found you playing with matches—an understandably dangerous situation. She felt a surge of anger and fear, rooted in an emotional wound from her past. Perhaps she lost something valuable or even a loved one in a fire, or was scared by her own parents when playing with fire as a child. Overcome with emotion, she may have given you the impression, or even told you outright, that what you were doing was "bad" or "wrong." She may even have felt it was her duty to scare you into understanding the very real danger of fire.

As a result, you may have expanded on this parental message and formed certain beliefs based in the context of this experience. For instance, as you played, you may have been imagining yourself running a scientific experiment or engaging your curiosity about the seemingly magical way matches "create" fire. But since your mother scolded you and said this was bad, you may have begun to equate this kind of curiosity with a feeling of fear and shame. And those feelings may have followed you into adulthood. Now, when an opportunity arises that requires curiosity, creativity, or exploration, you may become fearful, yet not even remember or know why. This kind of mixed emotion happens at the subconscious level, and as a result you may begin to lose trust in yourself and your own judgment.

In my previous book, *The Mastery of Self*, I tell a story about a child who is eating lunch with his grandmother. In an earnest and well-meaning effort to get her grandson to eat all the soup in his bowl, she tells him that wasting food is sinful. At first, he refuses to comply, but as she continues prodding, he relents and finishes the soup. When he is finished, she rewards him by telling him that he's a good boy. There is no malicious intent behind this punishment/reward system, but in his mind, the child now agrees that not eating all the food in front of him is a sin. He is domesticated to that idea, so he grows up approaching all of his meals through the lens of that agreement. This has the unintended result of him often eating all the food in front of him, even if his body tells him he is full and even if eating the extra food makes him physically uncomfortable.

Both of these examples make it clear that, when we are young, we listen to external voices like those of our parents and other caregivers, but very soon those voices become our own. Domestication becomes *self-domestication*. As my father says: "Humans are the only creatures on the planet that self-domesticate."

Once an agreement is formed in our minds, the original domesticator no longer needs to be present. We simply begin to reinforce our own domestication by developing our own internal dialogue. This is why domestication is so effective; once we buy into an idea, we no longer need anyone else to enforce it.

Very often, these internal voices add a chorus of negative beliefs to our constant self-talk, and they contribute to the mitote within us. Some of the voices are unique to each individual, of course, but several of them are so common that we can clearly identify them by name—like the parasite, the judge, and the victim.

The Parasite

The first and often the loudest negative voice in our heads—often the embodiment of all those good intentions in the process of domestication-gone-wrong—is what the Toltec tradition calls the *voice of the parasite*. The parasite takes the experiences of your past and amplifies the negative aspects of them, turning them against you in the form of self-judgment, self-rejection, and other forms of self-inflicted suffering. It is the active domesticator in our life.

In the current Dream of the Planet, the parasite's most powerful weapon is an idea that so many of us have come to accept in one form or another—the idea that *we are not enough*. The parasite delights in repeating this mantra over and over. *You are not smart enough, not attractive enough, not rich enough, not talented enough, not creative enough, not spiritual enough. You are not enough to warrant or deserve love, or acceptance, or belonging.* It's uncanny how many humans believe this idea at some level.

The parasite feeds on your psychological fear. It uses your past experiences, the judgment of others, and any other negative memories or emotions it can find to keep you small, obedient, or otherwise towing the line. The parasite is the voice inside your head that reminds you of past mistakes. It is the voice that convinces you that, if you show people who you really are, they won't like you, so you had better be agreeable and keep your mouth shut and your head down.

It's important to realize that the parasite is a master shape-shifter. Even after you have begun the inner work and are making positive changes in your life, the parasite will often pop up in new and unexpected ways. Even the spiritual path itself can become a trap used by the parasite to control and diminish you. For instance, I know many in the Toltec community who have fallen into the trap of believing that they are not being good enough Toltec Warriors!

So while it can be hard at first to recognize when you are being motivated by the parasite at any given moment, with time and practice you can learn to spot it. The fact is that anytime you hear a voice inside you that is using fear, shame, or guilt—even subtly—in an attempt to influence your actions, that's the voice of the parasite.

Like any physical parasite, the one in your mind feeds off its host. In this case, the parasite feeds on your past traumatic experiences, your domesticated fears, and the fears and negativity of others. Left unchecked, it eats away at your energy and power. If severe enough, it can actually begin to disable you. This is the case for people who have been living unhappy and unfulfilled lives for years, afraid to pursue what they really want and often not even knowing what that might be. The parasite within their minds has taken over and is running their lives. What could have been a beautiful dream has instead become a nightmare.

Yet there is good news. You can transform the voice of the parasite into the voice of an ally. This involves a monumental shift in perception, but the result is that you can use unconditional love instead of fear as a motivating force in your life. This is indeed a big part of the mastery of life—learning to heal the mind with love and acceptance. Through this work, and through the power journey outlined in this book, you can make the parasite your ally. You can teach it to thrive on creative imagination and joy instead of feeding on suffering and negativity.

In order to make this happen, you must understand the strategies of the parasite so that you can challenge its demands and make different choices, thus building up your personal power. Simply knowing that the parasite exists and feeds off negative energy and fear in your life can provide new insights for combating this fear and changing your relationship to it. By looking at how the parasite communicates with you and controls you, you can come to a better understanding of it.

The Judge and the Victim

The two voices, or manifestations, of the parasite, are what the Toltec tradition calls the judge and the victim.

Most of us are familiar with the voice of our inner judge. This judge, a master of self-rejection, speaks in both big and little ways. For instance, if you make a simple mistake like forgetting an appointment you made with a friend, your inner judge may prompt you to feel guilt. *I'm such an idiot. What's the matter with me? How could I be so forgetful?* These are small examples to which most of us don't give much thought, but it's important to note them as examples of the inner judge.

The larger ways in which you judge yourself are often easier to spot, but can be harder to let go. That's because they run so deep emotionally. For instance, if you get divorced or lose a treasured relationship, if you "fail" at a particular career or educational path, or if you made significant decisions when you were younger that you now regret, these can all be fertile ground for ongoing self-judgment. *I'll never recover from this hurt. No one will ever love me because I am unlovable. I'll never be able to make a living and support myself. My dreams are unachievable now. I am worthless.* And these self-judgments can poison you from the inside out.

Moreover, the judge has an audience without whom it couldn't exist. And while the voice of the judge is easy to identify because you've likely heard about the perils of this kind of relentless self-judgment before, you may not be familiar with its counterpart—what the Toltecs call the voice of the victim. While your inner judge is the voice that lashes out at every opportunity, the victim is the part of you that hears the voice of the judge and believes that what it says is the absolute, unshakable truth. The victim may even be silent when the judge speaks, but it is the part of you that feels all the emotions the judge creates—guilt, shame, worthlessness, and, of course, fear.

To be clear, this doesn't mean that there aren't situations in which you truly were a victim, but your goal is to get to a place where the fear of the past no longer controls you—a place where you can think of the past without being overcome with negative emotions that cloud your present. This means you have to recognize both the judge *and* the victim in your inner mitote. This can be some of the most difficult inner work to do, but your personal freedom lies right on the other side of it.

Sometimes you hear the voice of the victim in your mind without recognizing that the judge is there as well.

For example, the victim may bring up painful feelings from the past, causing you to experience frustration and hopelessness. *This always happens to me. I'll never get over this.* In this case, although you may not notice it, the judge is also present, condemning your actions or inactions in the situation at hand, as well as your actions in the past. Then the victim controls your feelings and behavior in the present by feeding on the negative energy of the past.

Another thing to notice about the inner judge and the victim is that the debt is never paid. In the outside world, in the legal systems of almost every place on earth, once a court case is decided (or finalized by the highest court in the land), the matter is closed. There may be consequences or punishment, but not more judging. In the court presided over by the inner judge, however, there is no such thing as a final verdict. Even the smallest cases can be relitigated, forever and ever, and the victim within continues to feel the pain of those judgments over and over.

For example, if I asked you right now to call up a tender memory of a time when you felt acute embarrassment, made a mistake, or hurt someone you cared about, could you think of one? Of course you could! No doubt, after recalling the circumstances of the event, even if it happened years or decades in the past, you will clearly hear the voice of the judge inside you, vivid and alive. You will probably even *feel* the emotional reality of the event all over again, complete with clammy hands, a quickening heartbeat, or an ache in your gut. The judge and victim work together in this way, and they hold enormous sway over both your physical body and your mental state.

Triple Play

And what does the parasite, through the voices of the judge and the victim, create inside you as they voice their opinions?

Fear, of course. They not only feed on fear; they also make more of it at the same time.

And herein lies the most detrimental aspect of these voices. When you give your attention to the voices of the mitote long enough, you begin to agree with them and use their unhelpful banter to form your very identity. Over time, you come to mistake these ideas and beliefs for your personal truths and see them as a part of who you are. This happens at both a conscious and an unconscious level. When this occurs, you may begin to see yourself as someone who "is just a failure," or someone who "will always be scared" because of something that happened to you in the past. Rather than recognizing these judgments as false beliefs, you now accept them as facts.

The Toltec Warrior endeavors to see that none of these statements are true. They are merely false agreements you've adopted to cover over the unique light, the nagual energy, that is at the true and authentic center of who you really are. The fear is real, because we feel it, but the trigger may not be real at all.

Don't beat yourself up about this—that's just more of the judge and the victim talking! These inner developments are natural and, frankly, nearly inevitable within the current Dream of the Planet. And let's remember the good news: Once you begin to recognize the voices in the mitote—the judge and the victim—you gain a powerful tool for mastering awareness. You can look around your own personal Sea of Hell, the chaos of swirling voices and judgments that follows you everywhere, and you can breathe in, then breathe out. You can say to yourself, or even out loud: "This is a lie."

Before you leave the Plaza of Quetzalcoatl, however, there is one more step you must take in waking up to the reality of your current situation. The mitote is a living nightmare, one from which we all need temporary safety and a place to rest. And that's exactly what we will explore in the next chapter when we consider the Island of Safety—even if it, too, is an illusion.

EXERCISE: IDENTIFYING YOUR MITOTE

In this exercise, you will make a list in your journal of the ways in which you experience the voices of your own mitote. Try to approach this like a scientist doing an investigation or a cartographer mapping out a new territory. Rather than diving deeply into memories that may be associated with the voices of your parasite, judge, or victim, simply make a list for further study. We will come back to this list later in your journey.

There are many ways to go about this. Here are some prompts to get you started if you're feeling stuck. Ask yourself the following questions:

- In what ways do I experience negative self-talk about my body? Examples: I think my nose is too big, or I am too short, or I am overweight.

- In what ways do I experience negative self-talk about my present or past relationships (or lack thereof)? This includes family, friends, and intimate relationships.

- In what ways do I experience negative self-talk about my career or finances?

- In what ways do I experience negative self-talk about my living environment?

Next, ask yourself what are the most significant traumatic or adverse experiences you have been through in your life? For example:

- I lost someone very close to me.

- I was physically/mentally/emotionally/sexually abused.

- I behaved in a manner I now regret and I hurt someone else.

You don't need to list every instance, just the ones that come immediately to mind. These are the ones often described as "life-defining" events.

Now, I realize that making a list of traumatic or adverse experiences can bring up negative emotions, even when you approach them with curiosity. But remember the radical acceptance meditation you did in the previous chapter. Everything that has ever occurred in your life has brought you to this moment. As you consider this list, remember that one of the goals in the mastery of life is to be able to revisit these instances in your mind without experiencing negative emotions. When this happens, you become free of these events, and naturally this is a process that takes time.

As you glance down your list, see how these self-critiques (which are almost always based on domesticated ideas with which you have agreed), combined with traumatic and adverse experiences, have been used to create parts of your identity. Consider how they contribute to the idea you have in your mind of who you are.

Is that identity true? Is that really who you are? Or are you someone far greater than anything on this list? Would you like to let go of the items on this list and experience yourself in a new way? These are the questions to consider as you progress on your journey.

And finally, if you hear your inner parasite talking loudly as you consider this list, try revisiting the self-acceptance meditation you did in the previous chapter.

Chapter 3

The Island of Safety

I have a friend who spent her junior year of college abroad in a place where she barely spoke the language when she arrived. After around three months of immersion in the history, art, and language of the place, she fell in love with a local boy. When she described this relationship to me later, she said that she felt as if, for the first time in her life, she had fallen in love as the "real her." And she felt that this young man had, in turn, fallen in love with her as a person free of the masks that she normally wore.

My friend had always been very smart and had done well in school. She could hold forth on almost any topic of conversation. At this point in her life, her sense of herself as an intelligent person, as a strong and capable person who could talk circles around others, was baked into her identity. It is who she thought she was. But when speaking a new language, she could no longer rely on complex vocabulary and grammatical structures. She struggled to communicate subtlety, humor, or sarcasm. She could not cloak her feelings or distance herself from her wants and desires. She became plain-spoken, simple, and free in a way she never expected. She communicated with an openness in her body and her face that was totally different from how she communicated in her native language. In fact, when her own mother came to visit, she was startled by the change in her daughter. In the context of her second language, my friend was a different person. Even after her relationship ended amicably, she always retained an expanded understanding of her own identity, which was wider than she had realized.

This was a lucky, inadvertent experience for my friend that led to the discovery of a couple of important lessons. First, she realized that we are different people in different contexts. How we think, what we believe, how we express ourselves, and how we form our identities all depend on our perspective and our collaboration with others. Our families, our education, and all the other cultural contexts in which we find ourselves influence how we behave.

But there is another, deeper truth hidden in my friend's story.

The Power of Illusion

In the last chapter, we discussed how the idea that we have of ourselves in our minds is formed in part through our individual fears and domestications as expressed by our inner mitote in our unique Sea of Hell. In the example above, however, we can see how our identities are also formed out of those activities and areas in which we excel. In my friend's case, her sense of identity, prior to her experience overseas, was heavily invested in her sense of being intelligent, confident, and well-educated.

But one of the biggest tasks you face on the journey to master life is that you must examine *all* the ways in which you create your identity. This is because the positive and negative aspects of those identities are, in fact, two sides of the same coin. Indeed, seeking solace in an identity based on traits you consider positive or "good" is a trap. When you do that, you are still seeking safety in an illusion.

Illusion in the Toltec sense may be a new idea for you. The Toltec tradition teaches that, even though your personal identity—what we call the "little self"—feels very solid, the truth is that it too is just a story you create and tell yourself. It isn't real. Like the beliefs you hold and the agreements you make, the story of *you* doesn't exist outside in the world. It only exists in your mind. And confusing that story with who you really are is not the path to personal freedom; it is a road to continued suffering. As you will see as we move through this journey together, most of the psychological fear you experience can be traced back to this false identity, or the story you have of yourself. That's why releasing your tight grasp on this identity is the key to not letting fear control you.

Other spiritual traditions have similar teachings. In Buddhism, one of the most fundamental concepts is *anatta*, which is often translated as "no self." The Hindu Upanishads teach that what we commonly refer to as the ego is an illusion of the mind. The more mystical traditions of the Abrahamic religions (Christianity, Judaism, and Islam) espouse similar ideas. Taken together, they all point to the notion that the idea of ourselves, what we often refer to as the ego, is not solid. And putting your faith in this illusion leads to suffering, not liberation.

This can be a difficult concept to grasp, and we will return to its importance throughout this book.

False Stories

On our journey through Teotihuacan, the Plaza of Quetzalcoatl symbolically represents the place where you create your identity—your story of your self. As we saw in the last chapter, this large open courtyard in front of the

Pyramid of Quetzalcoatl is home to the roiling Sea of Hell that is the mitote—the cacophony of voices in your mind that scream for your attention, including the parasite, the judge, and the victim. But in the center of this plaza, between the entrance to it and the pyramid itself, there sits a small, raised platform that Toltecs call the Island of Safety. This platform is the physical representation of the place where you seek refuge from the voices in your own metaphoric Sea of Hell—where you begin to develop defense mechanisms in response to what is going on around you.

The Island of Safety is where, in the formative years of your life, you decide which voices in the mitote you will listen to and which ones you won't. It is where you form agreements based on the beliefs, rules, and domestications you are taught. And it is also the place where you incorporate all the positive aspects of yourself into your identity—those personality traits you like about yourself, the activities and skills at which you excel, the accomplishments you've achieved, etc. All of these things come together on the Island of Safety to define your idea of you.

Compared to the Sea of Hell, this island offers a respite from the mitote and a sense of freedom and security. But the Toltec tradition teaches that this sense of security is also an illusion. There is no real freedom here.

Many of us, for instance, tie our identities to our professions, our material assets, our intelligence, our "good looks," our social or political affiliations, or even our spirituality. In most cases, we associate ourselves most strongly with a few dominant traits, and then cherry-pick those positive aspects of ourselves that feel especially important: *I'm a good father. I'm a successful professional. I'm a helpful citizen.*

Many of us have been taught to shore up our self-esteem and self-respect by building up these "positive traits" into false stories that become a part of our identities. In fact, much of the modern self-help movement encourages exactly this process. While on the whole this can be much better than the alternative of self-hatred and low self-worth, the mastery of life requires that you look deeper.

The goal of your journey to mastery is to see where you have *overinvested* in these good qualities or accomplishments to the point where they have become part of your identity. When you start to believe in these false stories, you set a future trap for yourself by making your self-acceptance conditional. You begin to think you are worthy only if you continue to succeed at these positive aspects in the future. This is not freedom.

To be clear, the Toltec path doesn't ask you to give up your best qualities or stop doing things that make you happy. What it asks is that you release the sense of identity you've invested in these false stories. Knowing the difference can be subtle. But your true value—as a single and unique expression of nagual energy—cannot be built up or torn down. It is perfect just as it is, which means *you are perfect just as you are*.

How can you tell when you've overinvested in a positive trait or activity? One good indicator is when you begin to feel superior to others because of it. For instance, have you ever been in a situation where you felt that your intellectual capability, or your career, or your material possessions, or your relationship status somehow made you "better" or "more important" than someone else? In that moment, you overidentified with this good quality or accomplishment to the point where it became a false story that then obscured your perception.

This is often easy to see in the case of our jobs and professional lives. Society teaches—and many of us are domesticated to the idea—that the jobs we hold can make one person more important than another. For instance, the president of a country may be perceived as "more important" than the janitor who cleans her office. Obviously, the duties involved in being president likely affect more people and perhaps require longer hours. But this doesn't make the individual "more important." Understanding the difference is key, because part of mastering life is recognizing that everyone on this planet has equal value; we are all part of the nagual. Thinking you are better than someone else is just as false and just as harmful as when the parasite in your mind says you are worse than someone else.

Furthermore, when you believe yourself to be better or worse than others due to some external achievement, you fall into the trap of comparison or competition. This is an endless cycle, a game that cannot be won, because the success or failure attached to this external accomplishment or reward becomes a condition for your own self-acceptance.

Whenever you form your identity based on these good qualities, you are inevitably comparing yourself to and competing against others, because the very notion of being "good" at something implies that there are others who are not good at it. And because the Dream of the Planet is based on constantly changing polarities, nothing in it lasts forever and you will inevitably be let down by any traits or accomplishments with which you've identified.

I know a very wise man who is in his mid-eighties. He lives in an assisted-living facility that he jokingly refers to as "God's waiting room." This facility is located in an affluent area of town, and he explained to me once that many of his fellow residents like to point to that affluence and talk about how important they used to be. In other words, they are consumed with telling stories about their past jobs, their careers, or their other accomplishments from earlier in life. As a result, he noted how many of their identities were tied up in the past.

Then my friend told me about another resident who he says never talks about her past in the same way. She is too busy painting, tending to her plants, taking walks in nature, visiting with loved ones, and doing other things that make her feel alive in the present moment. Unlike many of the others, he says, there always seems to be a spark of joy in her eyes. In fact, even though this woman is a few years his senior, she is teaching him how to stay young.

False Security

There are other ways in which we attempt to take refuge in this illusion of safety, and the mastery of life asks you to look deeper and see when you fall prey to them. For example, many of us have a deep fear of unexpectedly losing someone or something we love. In response to this fear, we may follow all sorts of unwritten rules to try to control people and situations in order to prevent this from happening. We may invent all sorts of "if/then" scenarios: *If I avoid taking any risks at work, then I won't lose my job and disappoint my family. If I stay the same size I was when we were married, then my partner won't leave me.*

Some even get angry with God when something is taken from them unexpectedly. They may feel that an agreement they were depending on was broken. *I did everything right, and still my loved one died, or my relationship collapsed.* The loss may feel like a cruel and personal betrayal, rather than part of the natural ebb and flow of life. Anger and resentment in the face of grief are understandable human emotions. But if, behind them, is the false belief that if you follow the rules, nothing "bad" will happen, then any sense of security you get from following the rules is an illusion, plain and simple. This is more common than you may realize, even for those who have been doing inner work for many years.

In fact, while you can and should take steps to protect your body and your loved ones by doing things like wearing seat belts or going for regular cancer screenings, the reality is that you cannot possibly predict the changes, including losses, that life will bring your way.

A similar way in which we try to create security and avoid loss is by trying to predict and control future events or other people. Many of us spend at least some time (or quite a bit of it) spinning out complicated scenarios in our minds about the future in an attempt to predict what will happen and gain an upper hand over the situation. This is especially common in the areas of finance, relationships, and physical health. *If I have enough money, nothing can hurt me. If I give my partner what he or she wants, my relationship will last. If I exercise and eat right, I won't get sick.*

Again, while it's good to plan for the future in all these areas, you'll want to learn to recognize when you have gone too far and are now trying to control the outcomes. Toltec Warriors know that all attempts at control are illusory and that, ultimately, they all originate in fear—fear of the collapse of the stories we have created.

The good news is that you can learn to recognize this psychological fear and view it as useful information. In this way, you use your fear as a helpful tool that can show you where you have a propensity to move from reasonable planning to attempted control of your world and its outcomes. Through practice, you learn to let go of the notion that you can and should build a wall of security to protect yourself. You recognize the difference between making plans and crossing the line into attempting to exert control.

Surrender

Once you have recognized that the false stories and the false sense of security you create on the Island of Safety are just illusions, you are ready to step off the island in search of greater personal freedom. When you make the decision to leave the island, you are saying to yourself that you are ready to question all the beliefs you have adopted about yourself and the world. You are ready to question the idea that your identity is fixed and real, that it is something that defines your worthiness. You are ready to relinquish control. You are ready for surrender.

In Teo, you express this willingness by leaving the Island of Safety and climbing to the top of the Pyramid of Quetzalcoatl. By doing this, you affirm your openness to move forward on the journey of the Toltec Warrior, a path toward self-realization and peace grounded in unconditional love and freedom from fear. By leaving the island, crossing the Sea of Hell, and climbing the pyramid, you make the first surrender on your journey.

Very often and especially in our current culture, we think of surrender as something negative. We consider it as giving up or losing something. In this instance, however, you are surrendering the idea that you can control people, places, and situations. You are surrendering any old beliefs that are manifestations of control. For instance, can you begin to release the idea that your looks, intelligence, or kindness are what give you value as a person? What would it mean to release the things that you think keep you safe? With each surrender of an old agreement, you are not losing anything so much as you are gaining— attaining space and opening to the potential to flow with the power of life in every moment.

Mastery is practice. Through practice, you learn to recognize your false stories—when and where and why you are forming them—and then to surrender them. By dealing with the underlying mental, emotional, physical, and spiritual aspects of your self (both positive and negative), you learn to approach life in a new way. You learn to surrender your false sense of security and your psychological fear and to live a life based on unconditional love. That is what we will do in the next five stops on our journey.

EXERCISE: IDENTITY LIST

As in the previous journal entry, in this exercise you will make a list. The goal here is to learn more about yourself and how you have created an identity. Writing with a sense of detachment, list any positive aspects of yourself or accomplishments that you use to establish your self-worth.

Here are some examples:

- I am generous, and I like to help people.

- I am a highly creative person who thinks outside the box.

- I have multiple advanced degrees.

- I worked hard and made sacrifices to become the successful person I am today.

- I am a good parent; my kids are happy and they get good grades.

- I am deeply spiritual.

- I am a physically attractive person.

When you are done with your list, spend some time considering how you would feel if something were to happen to take these aspects away from you. How firmly have you identified with these traits? Notice if you have overinvested your sense of self in them. Do you feel you need them to feel special or complete? Remember: You are already perfect exactly as you are, with or without them.

EXERCISE: LETTING GO

Surrender is difficult, and sometimes it's helpful to perform a physical action that grounds the change in your heart. This is where the power of ritual comes into play. Ritual is one way you can make emotional and intellectual exercises concrete by signaling to your body and mind that you are making a holistic change. This is a simple exercise, but it can be incredibly powerful.

For this ritual, you will need a small, ordinary stone. Don't spend too much time looking for the "perfect" stone—a plain old rock from your yard will do. Any stone that fits comfortably in the palm of your hand works well.

Once you've selected your stone, consider all the things you've listed in your journal—all the ways in which you've constructed your identity. Clutch the stone tightly in your hand, and imagine that all of the entries on your lists, both positive and negative, are going into the stone. Let any emotions you may feel move through you and into the stone in your hand.

Imagine that all of these feelings, stories, messages, and experiences are pouring into the stone, filling it with a multifaceted portrait of the agreements you have made. Don't rush this process; allow it to proceed until you feel intuitively that the stone fully embodies those agreements and that you are ready to let them go.

When you are ready, take your stone outside. This can be anywhere outside, in your yard or the nearest patch of grass. If you like, you can go to a special or sacred place in nature where you like to spend time. Spend a few minutes breathing deeply and feeling centered, with your feet planted firmly on the ground. Say either to yourself or out loud: "I am ready to surrender." Then drop the stone on the ground and walk away from it. Don't look back. Know in your heart that you've taken an important step on your journey to personal freedom. This is your symbolic equivalent to climbing the Pyramid of Quetzalcoatl.

Chapter 4

The Plaza of the Mind

I have a friend who was trying to stay fit during the COVID-19 pandemic, pushing herself with at-home workouts. While doing so, she injured her hip, but the injury didn't affect her daily life very much, so she mostly ignored it. She thought it would resolve itself. After a week, however, her hip was in constant pain. The ache was unpredictable and debilitating, showing up at unexpected times with no seeming relationship to her activities. She would start off on a walk, feeling fine, and have to call a friend to pick her up halfway through.

Going to physical therapy initially felt like a humiliating experience to her. She learned that the hip itself was so compromised that she couldn't do the most basic daily actions in a healthy way: walking, sitting, or standing. Her muscles had atrophied in some places and overworked in others to compensate for the injury, making things worse. She learned that the hip is central to any and every full-body movement. Desperate to get back to long runs and regular workouts, she had to scale back her activities to absolute basics. She had to relearn how to stand on one leg. She had to discover how to brace her core muscles just to sit in a chair. In order to start to heal, she had to isolate even the tiniest movements and find ways to do them without hurting herself.

My friend's story brings up a good question. How do we heal something that's broken when we have no choice but to keep using it? This was true of my friend's hip injury, but it is also true of the mind. We only have the minds that we have, equipped as they are with our own judgments, our domestications, and our traumas. The mind is the source of our perception. It's where the voices of the mitote capture our attention. It's where we form our identities. We have adapted to all of this, limping forward by masking the mind's dysfunction and making it work. But if we want to find true freedom—if we hope to run again—we have to learn to use our minds in a new way. It's no accident, therefore, that the next stop on our journey is the Plaza of the Mind.

In the Toltec tradition, the Plaza of the Mind is also called the Plaza of Temptation. We often think of temptation as being something outside of ourselves—that sweet treat sitting on the counter or the big bold letters of the sale price on an item we don't really need. But while outside forces like these may trigger feelings in us, the actual temptation already exists within our minds. If it didn't, these outside factors wouldn't affect us. This is why, in order to change our behaviors, we need to look first at our inner world.

The ancient Toltecs were very interested in the power of perception, thus they studied the human mind. They noticed that the mind is constantly telling stories, or what they called *dreaming*. When a person you've never met walks into a room, your mind immediately forms all kinds of judgments and stories about him or her. This person is attractive/unattractive. This person seems nice/mean. This person appears to be having a good/bad day. Of course, the stories your mind spins will depend on your own past experiences and your domestications. And, of course, they depend on how the event relates to the story you have created about yourself—your identity. Some of these stories may be fairly benign. But others, like some we will look at later in this chapter, can be harmful. Yet you can't just step outside your mind to get a clearer picture of reality. Your mind is the only tool of perception you have, and you can't engage with the world around you without it.

So when you begin a journey toward personal freedom, your first lesson is to recognize that your judgments and stories about reality are not always true, that you create them through the filter of your mind. When you recognize a story as a story, it begins to lose its power over you. This is important, because almost all your psychological fear is based in these stories. In the Toltec tradition, we call this healing process *mastering awareness*.

Mastering Awareness

Have you ever taken a familiar drive, perhaps going home from work, and arrived after thirty minutes or more of driving with the realization that you have almost no memory of the journey? You may remember some of what you were thinking about—a story from an audiobook or a conversation you had on the phone. But you don't have any memory of what the traffic was like, or whether or not the weather had changed. Of course, you made it home safely, so you know you had some level of awareness that enabled you to drive the car and respond to changing traffic conditions. How is this possible?

Our bodies have many levels of awareness, including many functions that don't require the thinking mind's involvement at all. In fact, much of the work of the body happens without our conscious commands (digestion, blood circulation, cell regeneration, among others). If we could feel all of the chemical exchanges that happen in our cells, or all the operations of our circulatory system, or every aspect of digestion, our minds would grind to a halt. These sensations would be so overwhelming that we wouldn't be able to do anything else. As a defense, we've developed the ability to use different levels of awareness for different tasks.

When you understand that there are thousands of other unconscious tasks being performed throughout your body in every moment, you can better see how the same can be true for the inner workings of your mind. Just as the cells in your body are performing their work without your conscious awareness, there are actions taking place in your subconscious mind of which you aren't aware. And these inner workings can, in fact, be just as powerful and important as your body pumping blood or healing itself from disease. In other words, it would be a mistake to think that, just because you aren't conscious of something, it isn't happening inside you.

Your main focus in the Plaza of Mind is to bring awareness to any ideas, beliefs, and stories that slip past your conscious mind, because it is these subconscious inner workings that drive you and influence the stories you tell yourself and the resulting choices you make. Some stories you may have told yourself for so long that you have forgotten they are just stories, and you may now mistake them for facts. To free yourself from this, you'll need to master your awareness.

So what exactly do I mean by awareness, and what does true mastery of awareness look like?

In mastering awareness, you seek to do two things: expand your perceptive capacities and then use this expanded input to understand your mind in a different way. This happens by noting and passing through these four levels of awareness:

Physical sensations. At this first level of awareness, you notice the flow of information coming into your senses from the outside—sight, hearing, smell, taste, and touch. What sensations are you feeling in your muscles and your bones? Breathe in and out and notice the sensations in your body as you do so. Notice the movement of your chest, the air moving in and out of your nose and mouth, any smells or tastes in the air. Try to take a few extra moments to perceive the texture of objects when you pick them up. Are they rough or smooth? Does the material feel harsh or soft? Tune in to your body and take note of any aches that you have been ignoring. Don't try to fix them; just be aware of them.

Thoughts and emotions. At this level of awareness, you begin to notice the flow of information through your mind's own personal dream. All of the raw information that flows into your senses gets processed according to this dream. Very often, however, you forget this fact. You become numb to these thoughts and emotions, or fail to be curious about them. It can help to create a visual cue to make you pause and notice your thoughts. For example, try to make a point of checking in with your emotions every time you walk through a doorway, or perhaps every time you take a sip of water. Alternatively, you can name thoughts as "thinking"—something often suggested by meditation teachers. If you can, try to notice when you are caught up in a train of thought and simply say (out loud if possible) "thinking." This builds your awareness of the fact that you are not your thoughts.

Reactions and stories. At this level of awareness, you begin to be aware of the larger framework through which you interpret your thoughts and emotions. Like your thoughts and emotions, these are your constant companions. Through the mastery of awareness, you begin to notice the reactions you have to others and the stories you tell yourself. In the latter case, you begin to find out if these stories are really true for you. This is the first step in learning to live life as a work of art—by choice, rather than by rote. Spend some time (one day a week) noting various habits in your journal. Engage in activities not unlike the mapmaking you've already done regarding your inner processes. You may already have noted a few of these inner stories that pop up regularly.

Unique perspective. This is the level of awareness that holds your always-shifting view of everything inside of you and in the outside world. Through building strength at this level of awareness, you increase your ability to change how you see things, to try out different contexts, and to grasp a deeper truth in paradox and the unknown. You soar up high like an eagle and gain vast perspectives. While this can be a difficult level of awareness to practice, it tends to emerge organically out of the development of the other levels described above.

In fact, each of these levels of awareness builds on the previous one. When you check in with your physical body, your breath, and your senses, you also begin to notice your thoughts and emotions. By observing and understanding these, you begin to notice the stories you tell yourself and find out where they came from. This allows you to challenge and change your habitual reactions and the stories that keep you small. When you step out of the comfort of these stories, you discover a wide new world of perspective, understanding, and knowledge.

Of course, this journey is never finished. Domestication is subtle and cunning, and some of your habits were formed a long time ago. You may be blown off track. You may change your viewpoint in the future. Don't forget the spiral nature of this work, in which you circle again and again through each of these levels of awareness, adding new depth and complexity as you go.

When you become more aware, the thoughts and beliefs in your unconscious mind can be brought to your consciousness. This can allow you to break free of old patterns like nothing else can. This deepening awareness can therefore result in changes in your behavior, which may be noticed by others before they are noticed by you. For example, I have a friend who, a few months after he started doing this inner work, went back to his hometown to visit his family. One night during dinner, his sister knocked over a glass and spilled its contents all over his lap. My friend laughed about it and quickly reached for a napkin to clean up the mess. As he did so, he looked up and saw that everyone else had a look of dread on their faces. "What's the matter?" he asked them. They explained that the "old him" would have lost his composure and become unpleasant at this type of event. My friend's family had noticed the change in him before he did.

In short, you will know you are making progress in mastering your awareness when you have a different response to the old situations and old temptations of your mind. Of course, you will keep getting dragged down by psychological fears from time to time, because the Dream of the Planet is full of emotional traps. But through awareness, you can learn to get up from any fall and gain another piece of wisdom. This journey takes time. Mastery is gained through the regular discipline of getting up again and again. The Warrior is born through action.

There are many other well-known tools for strengthening awareness, including meditation, mindfulness, breathing techniques, reflective exercises, journaling, and more. We will continue to touch on these throughout the book. Here, I want to introduce you to one way to strengthen your awareness that may be new to you.

Seeing the Story

One of the most powerful tools for strengthening your awareness involves noticing all the ways in which your mind tells stories. Our minds are very good at telling stories, but we often become unconscious of the stories we tell ourselves and others. It's like the automatic workings of our organs—the heart pumps blood, the kidneys clean toxins from the body, and the mind tells stories. The difference is that, unlike these bodily functions, some of the stories our minds spin can be unhelpful, even detrimental, to our overall well-being. When we bring conscious awareness to the stories we tell ourselves and others, we can see how they add to our identities. With practice, we begin to see the stories as just that—stories, not ultimate truth. Then we have options: we can release them, or we can consciously rewrite them.

But we can't rewrite or release these stories until we listen to what is really there. Only then can we go through the stories' details and begin to understand what makes them so compelling for us. And only then can we untangle our connection to them.

A friend came to my house the other day in an angry panic. A colleague had written him an email that seemed to indicate that she was losing faith in his ability, insulting him, and questioning his talent. I asked him what the email actually said, and he read it to me. In the email, his colleague briefly explained that she had overcommitted herself and needed to step back on a project that was important to my friend. She said she knew of someone else who would be brilliant at helping him, and she'd already checked that person's availability. He could step in and begin work on the project right away.

That was it.

No insults, no questioning his talents or losing faith in him or the project. And yet my friend had a detailed story running in his head. She doesn't think the project is good enough. She doesn't trust or respect me. She is pawning me off on someone else and trying to sabotage my efforts. Yet none of that was in the email at all. How did this happen? My friend filtered his colleague's words through his past history, his own insecurities, and his deep underlying fear of failure. In this case, the parasite was in control of his narrative.

We talked through the situation and, with a little awareness, he noticed that his heart was racing and his breathing was shallow. He noticed that he was feeling irrationally angry, and he admitted that, for him, this emotion often masked fear. I reminded him that, in the past, he'd told me that he sometimes fell into the trap of sabotaging himself if he felt that others weren't trusting and respecting him. Armed with all of these insights, my friend was ready to tell a new story about his colleague's message. He was able to feel grateful for her honesty about what she could and couldn't contribute at that time. He realized that he didn't have to take her decision personally or make other assumptions. And he could appreciate her recommendation for a new collaborator and knew he could count on her ongoing support.

The Power of the Jaguar

In my tradition, we often describe the awareness of a Toltec Warrior as the symbolic power of the jaguar. A native to what is now called Mexico, this sleek, muscular hunter can teach us a lot about how to turn on our senses and activate our emotional bodies. The jaguar stalks silently and tunes in to sounds, patterns, movement, and smells.

It keeps its focus narrow and wide at the same time, its body relaxed and ready. It notices when things feel different or strange. When its prey comes into view, it launches into powerful, decisive action. It doesn't know what the outcome will be, but it gives it everything it's got.

The jaguar is thus a good model for practicing awareness. In this case, your prey is the old stories and agreements that are blocking your quest for personal freedom. You are hunting down the thoughts, actions, and beliefs that keep these unhelpful stories alive and real for you. Imagine yourself as the jaguar of your own mind. Wake up in the morning ready for the hunt. It may be helpful to decide on one thing you will stalk on a given day—perhaps negative self-talk or fear of failure. Or you may be in search of something you want more of, like joy or rest.

What does this look like throughout your day? Perhaps you look in the mirror and your attention goes straight to some part of your body that you think is flawed. The jaguar wakes up in this moment and listens closely for what happens next. Your mitote kicks into gear. *I shouldn't look like this. If I were truly enlightened, I wouldn't care how I looked.* Then the jaguar, your inner warrior, leaps into the fray and starts to challenge the agreements that led to these thoughts. It has heard the words *should* or *would*—telltale signs of parasite thinking. *What is happening right now?* it snarls. *What do you really feel?*

You tune in to your body—not the reflection in the mirror, but your actual flesh and bones. Whatever you feel there—achy, warm, tingly—is a hundred times more real than the voices in your head. Now you have a chance to change the narrative inside your mind. *My body is hungry, so I'm going to eat a nourishing breakfast. I feel sluggish, so I'm going to give myself the gift of a walk outside.* Throughout your day, you continue to stalk your negative self-talk, listening for *should* or *would*. You are ruthless yet loving. Remember: The parasite's voice does not diminish when confronted with another harsh or critical voice, because this is simply more parasite talk. But it will eventually yield to a voice that is relentlessly loving, gentle, and kind.

You can do this with any aspect of your own personal dream right now. And it's important to remember that this, like many other exercises and actions in this book, is an ongoing practice. For example, I recently discovered that I was holding on to obsessive thoughts about some of the goals I have for the near future. Of course, it can be a good thing to plan and set goals and work toward a dream. But in this case, my inner jaguar noticed that something was off. My thoughts were repetitive. And my parasite had subtly entered the conversation, implying false promises. *Only once you finally have* X, *will you feel* Y *and know you are worthy of* Z.

Why do you want to achieve this goal so badly? my jaguar hissed instinctively, challenging my inner voices. *Is your striving coming from a place of genuine desire or a place of fear? How long will you pursue a carrot on a stick with singular focus, blind to the landscape of opportunity around you at all times? Why are you attaching your worth and your happiness to some future outcome, instead of finding it now, in the present moment—the only time that actually exists?*

When I questioned myself in this way, my inner jaguar was able to guide me back to the nagual within and remind me that everything is perfect exactly the way it is. I recentered myself and let go of the need to achieve this goal. If it happens, that's wonderful; if it doesn't, that's wonderful too.

In the next few chapters we will look at the practice of awareness and transformation through the lens of each of the four elements, following the path through the Plazas of Water, Air, Fire, and Earth. Moving through these elements, and the inner states and outward processes they symbolize, can help you restore a healthy relationship between mind and heart. When your mind and your heart are in harmony, all of your other relationships have the potential to be in harmony as well.

EXERCISE: AWARENESS WALK

An excellent way to begin flexing your awareness muscles is to take regular walks in a natural setting. A relatively peaceful place like a city or state park with plenty of flora and fauna is ideal, but if that's unavailable to you, a quiet neighborhood street is just fine. Don't worry too much about the location. I have a friend who practices walking regularly in a nearby wooded park, and it provides plenty of peaceful opportunities for contemplation, even though it's located right next to the city airport! The main idea is to find an area where you can breathe and take in the world around you through your senses. Your walk can be as short as five or ten minutes, or as long as you wish.

Before you begin your walk, set your intention. Take a few deep breaths and try to let go of any worries about the future or nagging thoughts from the past. Be solely in the present. Try to keep your sense of awareness as open as possible. At first, this may be hard to do, and you may find your thoughts wandering the way they do in the beginning stages of a meditation practice. Don't beat yourself up if this happens, just gently bring your attention back to the present moment and the sensations of your body interacting with the world around you—the scents and tastes in the air, the feel of the breeze on your skin, the muscles of your body moving you forward, the weight of your hands at the ends of your arms, the sounds of birds, airplanes, other people.

If it helps, you can assign a specific sensation to return to when you find your mind wandering. For example, every time you notice that you've left the present moment and have stopped being fully aware of your surroundings, put your focus on the bottoms of your feet as they move over the landscape.

Remember: This awareness is not about making any kind of judgment. If you catch an unpleasant whiff as you walk past a dumpster or a stagnant pond, for example, try to see if you react with a story—*I'll bet nobody's collected that garbage in weeks! The city's garbage collection program is so negligent!*—instead of simply observing and moving on.

EXERCISE: STILLING THE STORY-TELLING MIND

This exercise can help you extend your expanding physical awareness into the realm of the mind and then deeper into the stories and beliefs that have become habitual to you over the years. It's even easier to become distracted in this work. The mitote works hard to sidetrack you with its many voices, so it takes practice to see where stories are being told and to uncover their origins. The goal is to develop and strengthen your awareness of your inner self so you can apply your judgment of various situations more consciously.

For this exercise, you'll need the lists you made in your journal at the end of chapter 2. Choose one of the examples you noted of negative self-talk. First, turn it around a bit in your mind and see if you can narrow your focus to the specific story being told. For example, take this unfortunately all-too-common message from the parasite: *I'm unattractive*. Then consider any of its more specific corollaries—too fat/skinny, too tall/short, imperfect skin, crooked teeth, etc. Next, determine some of the stories you may be telling related to this message. *I will never be good-looking enough to attract a life partner. I don't deserve love because no one would want to look at me the way I am. Attractive people have it easier in life than I do. I would finally be happy if only I were thin/tall/had better skin/hair/features.*

Now spend some time reviewing the list you made at the end of chapter 3, where you looked at the positive traits and accomplishments in your life that you have been using to build your identity. Look for the stories you have attached to them. For example, perhaps you had something like this on your list: *I am a spiritual person.* In this case, the story you tell may be: *I am better than others because I am on a spiritual path.*

Once you've identified one or even a few stories surrounding the messages you chose, see if you can pinpoint a few times in your life when you may first have been domesticated to that story. If you can't think of a specific time, that's okay. The work you're doing in this exercise is more about seeing the story itself and being aware of how your mind works.

Finally, spend some time with your story and try to see it as just that—a story. It's not a real fact of life; it's a construct, a belief. You can choose either to accept or reject it every time it gets told. Give yourself permission to reject this story and, at the same time, forgive yourself for having accepted it in the first place. Imagine yourself surrounded by a great golden light—the light of unconditional love. This light surrounds you in every moment. All you have to do is become aware of it.

EXERCISE: YES AND NO

This exercise helps you take a deeper look at how and when you accept or reject situations. The Toltec tradition recognizes that we are all the artists of our lives. Every time we say yes, something is created; every time we say no, something is not created. We often forget the power we have in every moment to make choices, and we get stuck in automatic habits instead.

Do you know when you are accepting something and when you are rejecting it? How often do you stop and ask yourself: Do I want to say yes to this right now? You can practice this first on small, seemingly insignificant, decisions and habits. *Do I want to say yes to using my dominant hand for most things, or should I try to strengthen my other hand with this task? Do I want to say yes to turning the same way on my walk as I usually do or take a new route instead?* Once you've practiced making choices on these and other small questions, try some bigger ones. *Do I want to continue doubting myself today, or do I want to set that aside? Do I want to be the victim in this situation or the Warrior? Do I want to hold on to this opinion, or do I want to let it go?*

It's okay to reevaluate your choices even when you know they have big consequences. For example, I know a couple who ask each other every day if they want to stay married. They do it mostly as a loving joke, but it also reminds them that they are saying yes, over and over, to their partnership. And that they always have the option to say no.

Consider making the way you say yes into a game. In fact, play may be the most powerful, yet most overlooked, tool we have in our emotional arsenal for growth and learning. For instance, there's a children's book called *Yes Day!* It is all about one day a year when parents say an enthusiastic yes to everything their children want to do. (Before your judge gets riled up, let me tell you that the grown-ups put a few basic safety rules in place at the start.) Ice cream for breakfast? Yes! That is what we're doing today! Turning all the furniture in the living room upside down? Why yes, that is my number one priority! This silly and fun day creates space for an important understanding for children and adults alike. We tend to follow the "rules" of life out of habit, but we always have a choice to say yes to them. Saying yes out of obligation, fear, or comfort can easily get you stuck in a rut. Sometimes you can go so far down this path of unconscious rule-following that, by the time you hit midlife, you don't even know what you really want anymore.

EXERCISE: MIRROR RITUAL

In the Toltec tradition, we use the mirror to teach an important lesson about how the mind works. That's because, whether we realize it or not, when we look out into the world, we see ourselves reflected everywhere, in everything and everyone. We see things we admire about ourselves, and we see things that we dislike. Very often, when we see something out in the world and have an emotional reaction to it, what we're really reacting to is this reflection of our own inner selves. The problem is, of course, that we often don't realize we are looking at our own reflections.

However, once you are able to realize this, you become able to recognize yourself in everyone else. All of us here on this planet are struggling with the same search for meaning and happiness; we all experience joy, pain, suffering, and love. But, even if you see reflections of yourself in all others and in the world at large, that doesn't mean you can control them. The only thing you are truly able to control is yourself, which is then reflected back out into the world, for good or ill. When you're able to see this truth, you are better able to navigate your relationships and your community with grace and respect. We are each other's mirrors.

In this exercise, you create your own small "mirror room." You can also do this exercise in front of the mirror in your bathroom if that's what is available to you. First, set up four mirrors in the four quarters of a circle in a small area where you know you won't be disturbed for at least thirty minutes. You can do this using pedestals or small tables. Then set a backless stool in the middle of the circle so you can turn around and gaze into each mirror in turn.

Once your space is set up, settle onto the stool facing one of the mirrors. Close your eyes and take a few deep breaths. On each inhalation, feel yourself becoming more aware of the present moment—the sounds, scents, and feelings of the space you are in. As you exhale, imagine all the tension in your body melting away into the floor. Take as many of these breaths as necessary until you feel you are in a calm and relaxed state.

When you are ready, open your eyes and gaze softly into the mirror in front of you—into your own eyes. You may hear the voice of your judge almost immediately telling you about how you look. This exercise isn't necessarily about that, but definitely pay attention and perhaps remember to work with some of what comes up in your journal later. For now, as you do in meditation, just hear the voices, then let them go. Keep looking into your own eyes. After a while, you may begin to see yourself differently. This is a trick of the eye, but it can be startling. Just observe; this is you.

Now turn and look into the next mirror and make the same observations. This is you. And the next mirror? This is you as well. Everywhere you turn, you see your own reflection. This is a powerful metaphor for your life as you move out into the world. When you look into another's eyes, you are seeing a reflection of yourself. This isn't a lesson in narcissism; it's a lesson in finding connection and realizing that each person you encounter is experiencing the same desires for happiness, the same despair, the same disappointments that you are.

Once you've turned full circle, close your eyes and spend a few moments integrating the information you have discovered. Consider that, if you are a reflection of others and they are a reflection of you, then your inner work is not just a gift to yourself; it's a gift to others as well. Think of one small part of this gift that you'd like to reflect out into the rest of the world—one way in which you can change your personal dream. Imagine this as a physical gift you give through your eyes. Maybe this is the gift of remaining calm in the face of chaos. Maybe it is the gift of self-compassion. Now open your eyes, look into the mirror, and give yourself this gift.

Because this is a powerful exercise that can bring up a lot of thoughts and feelings, you may wish to set aside some time for journaling immediately afterward. Or you may want to go outside for a brisk walk to help refocus and ground yourself in the beauty of the natural world.

Chapter 5

The Plaza of Water

For cultures all over the world and throughout history, water has long been associated with healing and emotion. You probably already know that 50 to 75 percent of the human body is made up of water. Water is therefore a fundamental part of our being. So it's no surprise that you are drawn to coasts, rivers, and even puddles on a rainy day. A warm bath can restore you in a matter of minutes. An icy plunge can wake up your entire nervous system. Rain, humidity, or dryness in the air all affect how you breathe and feel. We also know that all animal life on the planet began in the oceans, and your body still contains a similar level of salinity to that found in seawater. Inside you and outside you, water is life itself.

The Toltec tradition associates water with the emotions and the emotional body. Water thus holds powerful healing potential for the body and mind. It is also an important symbol of purification. Thus, in the mastery of life, water is seen as a powerful ally as you cleanse your mind of all past agreements and attachments and your false identities. This is an essential step on your journey. So once you pass through the Plaza of the Mind, you enter the Plaza of Water, which marks the first of four locations along the Avenue of the Dead that correlate to the four elements: water, air, fire, and earth.

In the last chapter, we touched briefly on the aspect of emotions in the practice of awareness. The parasite in your mind gathers all kinds of agreements to control and manipulate you, and many times the judge and the victim use their voices to trigger emotions within you. That is how the mitote controls your behavior. The voice of the judge tells you that you always fail in a certain way. The victim within you hears the voice and believes it, which produces emotions like sadness, guilt, or despair. And these feelings, in turn, influence or even control your actions.

Of course, emotions themselves are neither bad or good. But in your personal dream and in the larger Dream of the Planet, you can become emotionally reactive for reasons you don't fully understand and are too fearful to investigate. You can also become attached to these emotional states in ways that lead you to see them as part of your identity, in much the same way that you mistake your domesticated beliefs for part of your core self. In these reactive states, when you become deeply identified with your emotions, you can do great harm to yourself and others.

That's why, if you want personal freedom, you must take a close look at your emotions, so that you can heal yourself to live in peace and not fall into the trap of emotional reactions and outbursts. Instead, you must learn to let your emotions flow through you in a healthy and useful way. This doesn't mean that you will no longer *experience* negative emotions. It just means that, through awareness, you can come to a place where they no longer *control* you.

For example, feelings of anxiety and regret often reveal areas of domestication and activities of the story-telling mind, because they are focused on what "might happen" in the future or what "should not have happened" in the past. When you look closely at these emotions, however, you find that, in almost all instances, there is a story based in psychological fear that fuels them. The emotions are real, but what triggers them may not be. The solution is not to push your emotions down and pretend they aren't there, but rather to notice, feel, and investigate their source. What thought did you have that produced this emotion within you? Is there a domestication or unhelpful story at the foundation of these thoughts and feelings?

By applying awareness and attention, you can learn to recognize when an emotion comes from a domesticated belief or story, and then investigate what needs healing within yourself. It is often your perspective on a person, place, thing, or situation that you need to question.

Purification

The ultimate goal here is *purification*—a word that can feel loaded for some people, as if we are dirty, bad, or sinful and need to be scrubbed clean or sterilized. This is not the Toltec meaning of the word, however. For us, purification is more like release, or flow, or easing. It is bringing movement to a rigid body and mind, opening space through which love can flow.

Purification begins and ends through love because, of all the primordial elements, love is the most like water. Unconditional love and water give life to everything. They both wash away any dirt or soiled areas of your past. Both are always flowing and changing. Like water, love has no shape of its own; both morph to fit the container that holds them. The energy that moves your body and determines the state of your mind also exists in a state of flow. Purification then is the application of unconditional love that removes blocks and allows for the natural flow of emotions and energy through your body, heart, and mind.

The element of water is thus naturally attuned to issues related to your emotional body. And when I say *emotional body*, I refer to the part of you that swells with love when you hug your child or parent, the part of you that releases a flow of tears in grief or frustration at a great loss, the part of you that feels simple joy when spending time with your best friend or cherished animal companion.

Modern science has many explanations for the bodily processes that take place when we feel emotions—like chemical reactions in the brain, for instance. But you are, of course, an integrated creature with overlapping physical, mental, emotional, and spiritual aspects. Still, if you could separate out your emotional capacity for a moment, you could say it acts as a kind of bridge between your physical body and your mind, relaying information through your nervous system. This capacity is highly sensitive to hormones and touch, and to the control or release of emotional flow. So it's easy to see how water holds sway here.

It's also easy to see how some of the agreements and beliefs we have formed over time, especially in our younger years, can act as obstacles to the flow of emotions in our lives. We dam up our feelings; we numb ourselves into stagnant pools; or, by contrast, we overflow in great floods of overwhelming emotion. Ideally, this emotional flow is like a healthy river, with strong deep currents in some places and gentle eddies and shallows in others. When we learn to be the stewards and caretakers of this river of life, and to explore the infinite manifestations of love flowing through it, our emotional bodies become powerful tools for transformation.

Of course, many of us have never learned to use our emotions in this way. If anything, the dominant cultural idea in the current Dream of the Planet teaches us to shut down certain emotions. It labels some emotions as uncomfortable, or not to be trusted, or even dangerous. And this can become a self-fulfilling prophecy at times, since people with little emotional intelligence *do* tend to have dangerous emotional outbursts and reactions, or to suppress emotions in a harmful way. Because they don't understand their emotions, they can't begin to trust them—or anyone else's. The cycle then continues, as anything emotional comes to be seen as uncontrollable or threatening—as something that must be stopped or reined in.

Many of us have also been domesticated to the idea of putting "logic over emotions" when making decisions. This belief rests on the idea that any "real" problem or situation has a logical solution. Furthermore, it rests on the flawed idea that, once we understand the logical choice, we will always take the most reasonable action.

As much as you may like to think that you are a logical being who makes logical choices—that you can separate your thoughts and actions from your emotions—ultimately, you are deluding yourself if you believe this. Your emotions almost always influence your behavior. If you think you are making "rational" decisions without being influenced by your emotions, you are likely either unaware of your emotions or suppressing them. Your goal in the Plaza of Water is to learn how to honor your emotions without being manipulated by prior domestications into having an emotional reaction that causes unnecessary harm to yourself or others. This is how you bring your mind and your heart back into balance.

I Feel—I Am

In the Introduction, we talked about the power of words. This power is particularly evident when it comes to our emotions and the way we use language. For instance, when someone asks how you are today, you may answer in a variety of ways:

- "I am happy."

- "I am sad."

- "I am excited."

- "I am good."

- "I am bad."

- "I am nervous."

- "I am excited."

- "I am depressed."

Common colloquialisms aside, however, none of these statements are accurate. That's because they all begin with the powerful words "I am," which are then followed by a feeling. Thus, you are describing yourself as a feeling when it would be more accurate to say that there are feelings of sadness (or excitement or happiness) inside you. "I am feeling excited right now." "I am feeling sadness right now." This may appear to be a small point, but the difference it makes in your mind can be huge.

In the first example, you are signaling to yourself that you *are* the feeling inside of you. Over time, if you say that enough, it can become a part of the identity you construct in your mind. *I'm an unhappy person. I'm always nervous.* Most of us know people we might describe as "basically unhappy people." Sadly, that is likely how they see themselves as well. It likely reflects the stories that play in their minds, which have become self-fulfilling prophecies by being repeated day after day.

With a subtle change in language, however, you can acknowledge that you are experiencing an emotion in the moment, rather than making that emotion part of your identity. And this brings us back to the concept of purification—to seeing emotions as akin to freely flowing water. Through purification, you allow emotions to pass through you without being blocked by your need to hold on to them and claim them as part of your fundamental nature, your true self. Your emotions are real, but they are not who you *are*. And you don't have to take action based on them—although sometimes you may, after assessing the situation and your inner reaction, *choose* to take action. This act of conscious discernment rooted in awareness is what makes you a master.

Emotions and Past Trauma

Your physical senses and your imagination both contribute to your emotions. Thus, experiencing real pain in the moment may not feel different from something that you are remembering. Your body may recreate the emotional experience, forcing you to live through it over and over. This is why grief and depression can be physically painful long after the event that caused them is past. This is also why emotional trauma can lead to physical ailments. And this is why perhaps the most important work you do with emotions must take into account the profound processes involved when you experience trauma.

When I use the word *trauma* in this context, I, of course, am referring to all the horrific events, abuses, or betrayals that the word commonly denotes. But I am also referring to much "smaller" injuries—those events that could be described as adverse experiences (rejection, embarrassment, failure to reach a highly desired goal, etc). Virtually none of us reaches adulthood without being touched by these experiences in some way. The emotions associated with these traumas are often the same no matter the circumstances, and the hurt they bring can have incredible staying power. We replay traumas over and over in our minds, and our emotional bodies continue to experience the pain. Some people go into a deep avoidance or even a self-protective denial about trauma because the memory of it becomes a reinjury.

It is possible, however, to remove the emotional power of your past traumatic experiences so you can talk about them freely, perhaps even to help someone else who is going through a difficult time. Indeed, it is critical to the path of mastery to uncover and release any old emotional pain that keeps you from experiencing personal freedom. This is part of the purification process I referred to earlier in the chapter. The goal of purification is to allow your emotions to run freely again, but at the same time to utilize the awareness you learned in the Plaza of the Mind so that they don't control you.

Among those who embody this kind of powerful work is Elizabeth Smart, the victim of a tragic kidnapping who now travels the world speaking out on the evils of human trafficking and the importance of self-worth for girls and women. Or Malala Yousafzai, who was shot on her way to school and eventually awarded the Nobel Peace Prize for her advocacy of education for women and girls. How is it possible that anyone who has experienced the kind of hell these women went through can transform their past trauma into service to others? Their outreach is directly related to their emotional pain. How can they revisit that pain and do their work without reinjuring themselves over and over?

"Forgiveness is something you do for yourself," Smart has said. "If I hold on to my anger for them [her kidnappers], it takes away a part of my soul. Forgiveness is giving up the hope for a better past. I do forgive them. I never want to see them again, though."

And Malala has a similar message: "I do not even hate the Talib who shot me. Even if there is a gun in my hand and he stands in front of me, I would not shoot him. This is the compassion that I have learnt from Muhammad the Prophet of Mercy, Jesus Christ, and Lord Buddha . . . And this is the forgiveness that I have learnt from my mother and father. This is what my soul is telling me—be peaceful and love everyone."

Healing Forgiveness

In the face of any kind of traumatic experience, however, forgiveness takes a lot of work. And the first step is to forgive yourself. In the two examples above, it's easy to see that neither of these young women were at fault for what happened to them. Yet when it comes to our own experiences, even when we have been victimized, we often carry feelings of guilt and remorse. Forgiveness starts with bringing awareness to these feelings in a safe place, with professional help if needed or desired.

Forgiveness requires being willing to go into your current emotional experience, to look at and accept whatever you are feeling, and then to forgive yourself first. Forgive yourself for your self-harming dream, for your mistakes, for not knowing better, for anything and everything. Remember: You are not forgiving for the benefit of whoever or whatever hurt you. You are forgiving in order to release the hold the emotions have over you, so that your pain doesn't dictate your actions in the future.

Forgiveness elevates your perceptions of what happened to you from the level of victim and perpetrator to the transcendent point of view of the eagle. From here, you gain a wider perspective. This allows the wound to heal so that, when you revisit it, it no longer reinjures you. If an emotional wound is left open, and/or if you reopen it whenever you are reminded of it, there is a part of you that is saying yes to that wound, a part of you that still wants or needs it to be raw and painful in some way. This is sometimes a very difficult thing to realize and accept, but it can be incredibly powerful to take a deeper look at how keeping a wound open may actually be serving you in some way. It may be that you are keeping it open until you are truly ready to heal, or perhaps you have made it a part of your identity. That's okay. Forgive yourself for that as well. But you can always choose to start the healing process, at any moment.

Often, talking to people you trust and sharing your feelings with them open the door for healing. When feelings are taboo, when you think they should not be discussed or even admitted to, you shut down the chance to work with them. As the great Fred Rogers reminds us:

"When we can talk about our feelings, they become less overwhelming, less upsetting, and less scary. The people we trust with that important talk can help us know that we are not alone."

Your emotions offer an enormous wellspring of material with which and through which you can work on your journey to personal freedom. Your emotional body is linked to a veritable library of stories, beliefs, agreements, and memories you can examine in your work as a Toltec Warrior. And your freedom often lies right on the other side of a painful emotion.

Healing Laughter

Ironically, comedians are often known for being miserable in their offstage lives. Although it seems like a contradiction at first, this actually makes a lot of sense. Often their struggle with painful childhoods, past traumas, depression, or addictions led them to develop humor as a tool to divert the attention of others to where they wanted it to go. Or it may have become a way to cover over their own tender spots with a protective shield of one kind or another. Comedic genius Dave Chappelle talks about how he avoided being teased and bullied as a child by calling out his own faults before anyone else could and making people laugh at them. Humor allowed him to control the narrative. This is a perfectly good survival strategy for the victim child, by the way. There is nothing wrong with donning a mask of comedy to stay alive, stay safe, and protect yourself.

The problem often comes later for people who have had to adopt this mask early in life, because the mask itself later becomes painful, even crippling, to wear. In the middle of their careers, some comedians have to change from being self-focused to other-focused. Their style of comedy may remain the same, but the impulse behind it changes. The things they did as children and as young adults to be funny were done less out of choice and more out of necessity. But with a little perspective, comedians can come to see their role in a different way. They can come to see their humor as being in service of something bigger—a gift to their audiences and to others in their field. Their survival strategies become gifts.

When you're able to laugh from a genuine place at a past embarrassment or hurt, that's a sign that you are healing. When you can laugh at situations that you used to take very seriously—and for which you may judge yourself—this is an indication that you're no longer using those situations to form an identity. When you still view past events so seriously that you aren't yet able to laugh at them, that can indicate where you still have work to do.

Part of the work of unblocking the river of our emotional lives is to allow the flow of joy. It is interesting that, even when we pretend to laugh when there's nothing we find funny, this can often transform into authentic laughter. This is especially true when practiced with others. This is the phenomenon at the heart of laughter clubs and laughter yoga, where people get together to practice a series of laughter exercises that very quickly transition into delightful, contagious, real mirth. There are even some amazing videos on YouTube of strangers starting "laughing attacks" on crowded subways or buses.

My point is that, sometimes, we don't let ourselves feel the good things. Perhaps we think that if we shut down our positive emotions, we can somehow ward off the negative ones. But it doesn't work that way. We don't have a "good-feelings" emotional body and a "bad-feelings" emotional body. They are one and the same.

So practice feeling sadness. Practice laughing. Let the tears and the laughter flow. Neither one defines you.

Two Wolves

You may have heard this story of the grandfather counseling his grandchild.

"Inside each of us two wolves exist," the grandfather says, "one a wolf of compassion and the other a wolf of hate and selfishness."

"Grandfather," the child asks, "if they fight, which one will win?"

"The one you feed," the grandfather replies.

I loved this story from the first moment I heard it, and I was sure at the time that it was telling me to feed the wolf of love within me. Then, after a while, I realized that the story tells me that *both wolves exist in me*. Both wolves exist in all of us. Unconditional love, then, is not choosing to ignore or destroy the hate or selfishness within us; it lives in the willingness to see and love *all* of ourselves.

Conditional love sees only what it wants to see. But with awareness, with knowledge, you learn to see both the darkness and the light. It's like the concept and symbol of yin and yang—two halves of a whole, equal, separate, intertwined, and each holding a piece of the other within itself. You are both wolves; you contain both sides of almost any opposite qualities you can imagine. But you do not allow them to be at war with one another.

I accept me as I am now; I am both wolves. To love myself is to feed both. I choose, however, not to make them fight; the war ends with me. When I have this peace within, unclouded by conditional love, I approach myself and all my relationships differently.

Practice saying "I love you and I accept you" to everything—inside of you and outside. Absolutely everything. You do not have to like what you accept; you just have to acknowledge it. Let the pure rushing water of your emotional body flow. Fill your cup with unending, unconditional love.

EXERCISE: THE EMOTIONAL BODY

Working with the emotions can be intense, and journaling can be particularly helpful when working through them.

Begin by considering what domesticated ideas you may have acquired over the years concerning emotion. Perhaps you've been told that you're too emotional. Or perhaps you've been domesticated to believe that logic is always more important than emotions. What do these domestications mean for your emotional body? How do they limit you? Do you "trust" your emotions? If not, what might you be missing? Write out your thoughts and feelings around emotions. And remember: This isn't work you ever have to show anyone, so feel free to be honest and expressive.

The key is balance. You are learning to recognize when the parasite has hijacked your emotions to keep you living in psychological fear, while at the same time allowing those emotions to flow through you. The goal is to let your emotions guide you to find and release these domestications by ceasing to believe them and making conscious choices.

A teacher I met in Sacramento once taught me what forgivness was: "Forgiveness is the moment you no longer wish the past were any different, you accept that it happened and you let it go."

EXERCISE: FORGIVENESS LETTER

Forgiveness can be a challenge for many. It certainly isn't something that can be rushed or forced. All the work you do in this book and on this journey helps to create readiness for the power of forgiveness, so don't worry if you don't feel you want to do this exercise right now; come back to it when you are moved to do so. And don't worry if you feel you want to repeat it again later, and then again after that. This is good and natural. We all have any number of things we need to work through and forgive.

Refer back to the work you did in previous chapters—particularly the lists you made in your journal in chapter 2 and the stories you examined in chapter 4. You may be able to see a variety of places that would benefit from forgiveness, either for yourself or for others. Choose one of these to work with. You can start with something relatively simple and straightforward. Building up to more challenging work is just fine.

When you have the person, situation, or condition clearly in mind, write a letter in your journal explaining the pain you've suffered or caused and offering your forgiveness for it. If you are working with self-forgiveness, address the letter to yourself. Here is a suggested format:

1. Describe the incident—what happened, where, and who was involved.

2. Explain how you felt at the time of the incident and how you feel about it now.

3. Offer forgiveness (including self-forgiveness) and explain why. Please remember that forgiveness is for your benefit, not anyone else's.

Be sure to take your time. You may even want to work on different sections of your letter at different times. When you complete the letter, acknowledge to yourself that you are ready to move on with your life and that you don't want this incident to hamper or control you, or become an identity for you. When you think of this incident in the future, you may still have emotions come up, and that's completely normal. Allow those emotions to flow through you, and then remind yourself of the letter you wrote and that the act of forgiveness is for you.

EXERCISE: TOLTEC RECAPITULATION

We spend an enormous amount of time and energy holding on to situations and experiences that have hurt us in some way—so much so that we actually create a deficit in the amount of energy available to us for other more joyful things in our lives. This breathing practice, called Toltec Recapitulation, allows you to go back to an event in your mind's eye and reclaim any energy you may have left behind.

This technique uses the universally recognized power of the breath to cleanse the negative emotions from memories. Its purpose is to reclaim the emotional energy you invested in an experience so that you can recall it *without reliving it*. When there is no emotional charge left to a memory, it is neutral and can no longer be used to generate suffering inside you. Thus you can take back your emotional power so that you can move forward and heal the open wounds that remain from other painful and traumatic events in your past. This practice can be done any number of times to address painful experiences.

Begin by remembering a specific time when you experienced a deep emotional wound. Perhaps there is something on the list you made in chapter 2. This may be a time when you were physically, mentally, or emotionally abused. Perhaps it was the end of a marriage, the death of a loved one, or a major physical accident or illness. Choose an experience that brings up negative emotions when you remember it. This can be difficult, so take your time.

Find a quiet space where you can either sit comfortably or lie down undisturbed for several minutes. Take a few moments to recall the incident you have chosen in your mind, or write out the details of the event in your journal. Then begin by inhaling and exhaling deeply. As you do so, focus on the memory and allow all of the negative emotions you experienced during the event to come up within you.

Notice how the emotions move in your body. You may feel your skin flush or experience a fluttering in your stomach. These are physical manifestations of emotional energy. Consider the many times you have replayed this event in your mind, using the emotional energy behind it to hurt yourself or others. As you inhale, draw this energy back to yourself; it is yours, and you have the right to choose where you wish to use it going forward.

Now exhale, keeping the memory clear in your mind, and imagine that your body is pushing out and releasing all the negative emotion you feel toward the event. Exhale your sadness, your shame, your fear, your guilt—any negativity that arises when you think of this experience. The event itself is in the past. It cannot hurt you any longer.

Keep breathing in this intentional way as you think about the situation or event. As you inhale, draw your energy back; as you exhale, push out any negative emotions. Continue until you feel that you have reclaimed all of your energy and expelled all the negativity. It may take several sessions to work through a single event or memory. This is perfectly normal. Just do as much (or as little) as you feel possible in each session. With practice, you will eventually be able to summon the memory of the experience without reliving it emotionally. When this happens, you will know that you have successfully released its power over you. Your energy, your power, is now fully yours again.

EXERCISE: CONNECTING WITH WATER

Here are a couple of simple suggestions that can help facilitate your connection to the emotional flow and healing nature of water:

Take a ritual bath. If you have access to a bathtub, create an evening of relaxation and cleansing by setting aside some special time to take a sacred, healing bath. Light candles, add flowers or other natural items to scent the water, play soothing music, and allow your body to relax completely.

Visit a natural body of water. Work to see this body of water in a new way. Lakes, rivers, and oceans all have uniquely beautiful energy when we take time to notice it. Activities that can help you connect to the healing power of natural water include swimming, dipping your hands in the water and splashing your face, singing to the water, or sitting in silence while listening to the water's natural music.

Chapter 6

The Plaza of Air

Whenever I am trying to finish a big project, a class or presentation, or even a book like this one, at a certain point I inevitably find myself stuck. My initial excitement has worn off. My readiness to show up and get the work done is still there, but it only gets me in front of the screen or the paper, and no further. I sit looking at the words and my mind goes into a fog. I know that my thoughts are there, somewhere in the mist, but I don't know how to access them. Then, I hear a still, small voice inside me: *Get up*.

I have gotten better about listening to this voice, even (or especially) when it doesn't make logical sense to me. *Put on your shoes*, it says. *Go outside*, it says. And so I do, even as the parasite voice inside me starts chattering away. *This is useless, where do you think you're going? Books don't write themselves while you walk around outside!* I laugh and say out loud: "Who knows? Maybe they do." I find that joking with my parasite voice can undercut its power in my head.

As I breathe in the outside air, I feel my body lighten. I feel the sun creating a lovely warm tingling all over my skin. My feet fall into a rhythm, and I try to clear my mind of any particular destination or plan for my walk. I am not trying to think about where I got stuck or why. Instead, I am stalking something else—the clarity of vision I need to continue creating.

Soon, I begin to hum—perhaps a song about a sunny spring day, or perhaps just a song that I love. I hum quietly at first, walking along with the rhythm of the song. I can feel my mind start to reorient to the world around me. I see details I didn't notice yesterday. I hear a birdsong that hasn't been around since this time last year. I marvel that, just moments ago, I sat paralyzed in a dense fog of my own making. I begin to sing. I have always loved singing. It feels precious to me, and makes me feel a little vulnerable, as if I were bringing up a precious jewel from inside me and offering it to the world. Just giving it away. I keep walking.

Soon, I am that crazy man you see on the street, singing his heart out and striding happily in the sunlight. I don't care what anyone thinks, and I'm not worried about the project that awaits me back at my desk. I am taking deep breaths in and out to support the song. Then it hits me. I know what I have to do; I know the next step I have to take or the next idea that has to go on the page. It's a stroke of insight that's crystal clear. I practically run back to the house to get it down.

Perhaps you have your own version of this story—a place you go or a simple action you take that parts the clouds for you and provides space for your vision to move you forward. If not, then please view this chapter as an invitation to find one, because this is the feeling you are after as you enter the Plaza of Air on your journey toward the mastery of life.

Inspiration

Air is directly connected to the breath. Like the nagual, air is necessary for our bodies to thrive. Thus we can say that air is the inspiration for life. In fact, the word *inspire* comes from a Latin term that means "to breathe in or blow into." As breath fills our lungs, it inspires us. Breath is life itself, and inspiration and creativity are acts of life.

The element of air also represents your spirit—the part of you that can't be measured on a scale or with a ruler. It's the part of you that is your unique manifestation of the nagual energy. In your journey so far, you have been dealing largely with things that have caused problems in your life: domestication, trauma, the mind, clogged emotions, and how these feed your psychological fears. There is ongoing work to be done in all these areas. But in the Plaza of Air, you pause to renew yourself and reconnect with the nagual energy. This brings you clarity and focus, opens up your perspective as to what is possible for you, and aligns your vision and inspiration to the spirit of life itself.

The Plaza of Air is where you hone your craft as the artist of your life, so that you can be ready when life offers you opportunities. Once your vision is cleared of the muddiness of old agreements and habitual traps—once you have mastered awareness—you are free to make decisions and follow new paths based on your true preference or on simple curiosity. This makes you ready to say yes to life in a new way.

I once heard an art history teacher say that every revolution in art is a return to realism. How can this be true? Cubism, abstract art, impressionism—none of it looks like "real" life. I think what she meant, however, is that each new generation of artists arrives at its own awareness of how to represent reality in ways that feel most real to them.

Likewise, when we begin to create the masterpieces of our own lives, we draw on an innate desire within each of us to express ourselves in new and authentic ways. Remember: The word *Toltec* means "artist." And the element of air is connected to clear vision and creativity. It invites us to express ourselves by trying out new and creative things.

Unfortunately, some of us have been domesticated into believing that we don't like certain things without ever having tried them. These things may have been forbidden or ignored in our own childhoods or personal histories. These domestications may have been part of the "artistic style" of our parents and others who raised us. But it is important that we test these beliefs for ourselves to find out what is actually true for *us*. In this way, we can achieve an artistic revolution within ourselves and pioneer a whole new genre of self-expression.

For instance, a friend of mine grew up in a family with no music or dancing. It wasn't forbidden; it simply wasn't there. No one in his immediate family enjoyed these things. As a result, he didn't feel any attraction to either music or dance, or even consider the idea that he might enjoy them, until adulthood. Once he started the awareness practices covered earlier in this book, he noticed that watching other people enjoy music intrigued him. He began to question the lack of music and dance in his own life, and he decided he wanted to learn how to play the guitar. He booked himself some lessons and soon found that he enjoyed it very much. His new appreciation for music opened up a whole new world for him. It brought a level of creativity, joy, and presence into his life. It connected him to his physical and emotional bodies. His musical ear developed, and he started to listen to many different kinds of music. He even started to hear the normal daily sounds around him in a new way.

Your awareness feeds your creativity and provides inspiration that evolves over the course of your life. Questioning your domesticated identities, expanding and growing into new areas, becoming aware—these are key features of the personal freedom you seek as you progress toward the mastery of life.

Infinite Possibility

The notion of infinite possibility is another idea connected to the element of air. Think of the feeling you get when you are standing high up on a mountain peak looking out over the landscape. You can almost see the curve of the earth itself, as the wind whips past your ears in a roar. Think of how different your sensations are in this airy space from what you might feel burrowed into the earth in a warm underground nest. Or what you might experience swimming in a cool, placid lake. Each of these feelings is important and valuable; the key is to know when to use the tools of each element. You can call on air to support you when you want to master the possibilities presented to you in life.

Recently, while hiking in the mountains near my home, I came out onto one such overlook. A deep, wide valley stretched out below me edged by high mountains on either side. As I approached the edge of a drop-off to get the best view, a hawk rose up swiftly into my vision, swept on a strong updraft. It soared high above my head within seconds. I watched it play in the wind, catching currents and gliding this way and that, or just hanging for long moments in the sky above the valley. I noticed how it made slight adjustments to its wings and body in order to remain steady in the gusting wind. If it hadn't been so skillful, it surely would have been dashed against a cliff or forced to land.

The hawk made it all look so easy. But the truth is that mastering something, even what you may be born to do, takes time. The circumstances of life are always changing. Staying still may look simple or easy from the outside, but if you're honest with yourself, you know it takes a lot of work to be in balance and to stay where you want to be in your heart and your mind.

I have a friend who took an early retirement that was offered to her, because it seemed too good an opportunity to pass up. After her initial sense of freedom wore off, however, she found herself at a crossroads. Old agreements about what it meant to "be old" or "retire" crept into her daily thoughts, and soon she was regretting her decision. She felt that the road of life ahead of her was short and going downhill. Then, she had a burst of clarity. There were so many things she wanted to do with her life, so many projects that she had long ignored or pushed aside. She remembered that none of us knows how long the road ahead of us will be. But she also realized that, right here in the present moment, that road is the longest it will ever be. She got busy saying yes to the infinite possibilities of her life.

The Plaza of Air invites you to look within and make sure you are really living the life you want to live. If not, why not? What can you do to change it? And if you truly cannot change your circumstances, how can you change your mindset about them? What other opportunities are available to you in light of these circumstances? What is your potential?

Potential is a fascinating concept and one that is not easy to understand. Perhaps you cannot and will not be or do all the things you may want to be or do in your lifetime. Thus, in a sense, you could say that your potential is limited in relation to life itself. On the other hand, you really have no idea what your own potential is. In fact, I would argue that those who think they know their own or someone else's potential are probably stuck in a false belief. While you may indeed have limits, the truth is that you do not know what they are.

The seeds of every possible future are all around you in the present moment. In the teachings of my family, we say that there is no outcome that can exist in the future that doesn't already exist in some potential right now. You've already learned about stalking old behaviors and transforming them. But you can also hunt out these seeds of potential, these tender shoots. You can be clear about what you are looking for. And you can have the vision to see where they exist right now, even if they feel almost invisible to you. Then you can cultivate and nurture the future you desire. Today, you are the youngest you will ever be and you have your whole life ahead of you—how do you want to experience it?

Unconditional Gratitude

The Toltec tradition teaches that every breath we take is an expression of our gratitude for life itself. We breathe in inspiration, and we breathe out gratitude. Remember: Even when you are not aware of your breath, it is still happening.

To see infinite possibility and be inspired in the present moment, however, you will want to learn to develop gratitude for everything. In some ways, this is easy. We are often grateful for our loved ones, for the good news we receive, for our own health and safety. Most of us are readily grateful for what we have agreed is "good" about our lives. But in the quest for personal freedom, can you also be grateful for the job you *didn't* get or the relationship that *didn't* last? Can you feel gratitude for wounds and losses and threats? All these experiences hold both "good" and "bad" within them. And your gratitude, like your love, can become unconditional.

For example, when the global COVID-19 pandemic first began in 2020, many people were faced with a huge surge in their normal fears and anxieties. Maybe these emotions were not always for themselves, but certainly for their loved ones—elderly parents, friends, colleagues. The fear that people would suffer and die was very powerful and very real. I know one woman who became obsessed with protecting her elderly parents from the virus. She wanted to control their every move. And her fear was bleeding over into their lives, making everyone miserable. But again, fear can be a great teacher.

My friend complained to me that her parents were chafing at her help and getting annoyed with her. They had snapped at her more than once on the phone. She thought it was because they were afraid. I suggested that it might be because *she* was afraid, and that she was spreading her fear out in front of her wherever she went, like a big cloud of dust. I told her to take a moment before she got on the phone or texted her parents to call on her discipline and training. I encouraged her to, literally and figuratively, clear the air by taking some deep breaths. Breathe in. Breathe out. I then pointed out that she could be grateful for this fear, that she could acknowledge it and explore its deepest core through gratitude.

"What do you think might happen?" I asked.

"I'm afraid they will get sick," she admitted. "I'm afraid they will die without me there. I'm afraid my kids and I will be left alone."

When I asked her to trace those fears to their roots, she found that her fears were actually based in love. We don't fear people dying unless we love them deeply, unless their presence in our lives brings joy and comfort. So I encouraged her to explore that love.

"I love my father and my mother so much," she realized. "I'm so grateful that both my parents have lived into my adulthood. I love that they are a huge part of my kids' lives."

I prompted her to be as specific as possible about the love underneath her fear—to breathe in gratitude for all those gifts from life, that love. Doing this before each of her interactions with her parents rebalanced her, and she found her communications with them around safety during the pandemic went much better as a result.

When you work with gratitude in this way, you don't eliminate fear. But you can strive to transform it by realigning it with a truer vision of the circumstances.

Living a fear-based life is like trying to care for a tree that is disconnected from its roots; it would, of course, fall over in the slightest wind. As spring approached, you would be desperate to hold it up, building all kinds of structures around it to provide support. But ultimately, these are just temporary fixes; they don't address the real problem. A tree needs to be connected to its roots, and *life's roots are always love*. If you are able to reconnect your own fears to their roots, to find their origin in love, you can transform the energy of fear—and let the tree of love burst into the bloom of inspiration, new life, and creativity.

Silent Knowledge

Clear vision is what helps you tap into and connect with your intuition. The Toltecs call intuition *silent knowledge*, a type of knowing that doesn't come from the logical, rational mind. Almost everyone has a story of a time in their lives when they "just knew" something that didn't make any rational sense at the time, but that was later revealed to be true.

While there is value in logic, the current Dream of the Planet holds it in such high regard that many of us have been domesticated to distrust the silent knowledge within us. The Plaza of Air is where you learn to ask yourself important questions about your relationship to this silent knowledge. How connected do you feel to your intuition? Do you receive messages from it and listen to it regularly? Or do you dismiss intuition as imagination, opting for a more logical approach? Learning to listen to and connect with the silent knowledge that is beyond your thinking mind is one of the key aspects of life mastery, so it is important that you examine any domesticated ideas you may have around this topic.

If you're feeling out of touch with your intuition, I have some good news. Your connection to it naturally improves when you do the other inner work covered in this book. By recognizing and releasing unhelpful domestications and the voices of the mitote, and by freeing up any emotional blocks you have so that your emotions flow, you open yourself to a type of knowing that has always been available, but that you may not have been able to hear. Almost any experienced Toltec Warrior will tell you that tapping into silent knowledge is one of the biggest benefits of this path. Intuition is perception that is uncorrupted by the story of the parasite. It is the truth that is percived by the nagual.

I am often asked how you know when a message is coming from your intuition and when it is coming from the fears of your little self. This can be difficult to discern at first, but I can tell you that it gets easier as you practice. Remember: It's practice that makes the master.

The other good news is that, by learning how to truly listen to yourself, you become better at listening in general. In this way, intuition is not only a gift to you; it is a gift to others as well.

EXERCISE: CLEAR VISION AND POTENTIAL

We are the artists of our lives, and yet we often get bogged down with other things and forget to do what makes our hearts sing. Or worse, if we are not skilled at cultivating our own joy, we may not even be sure what makes our hearts sing because they have been quiet for so long. The Plaza of Air invites you to change that and reconnect with clear vision and potential.

For this exercise, make two lists in your journal. In the first, list the things that you already know you love to do and that bring joy into your life—for instance, painting or drawing, playing a musical instrument or singing with others, hiking or camping, gardening, community organizing or volunteering, going to concerts, reading fiction.

In the second list, write down all the things you think you might like to do, but you haven't yet tried. For instance, have you always wanted to take salsa lessons? Put that down. Would you like to travel to India? Add that too. You get the idea.

Now look at the first list, the things you know you love to do, and compare it to the things you've actually done over the last month. How many things on this list have you done and how often? Sometimes we don't take the time to do the things we love. Being more aware of how you spend your time can prompt you to make adjustments. What items on the list of things you love to do can you schedule in the next month? Now look at the second list. What haven't you done yet that you can put on your schedule right now? Remember: You are the artist of your life. Make enjoying life the central theme of your masterpiece.

EXERCISE: STRENGTHENING YOUR INTUITION

You can strengthen your intuitive skills in simple ways that will serve you well. While some of your more powerful stories regarding intuition may involve major events, the vast majority of them are probably tied to minor day-to-day occurrences. By focusing on these smaller and less dramatic moments of intuitive decision-making, you can relearn how to listen to your inner silent knowing when more impactful decisions need to be made. Here is just a short list of suggestions for paying attention to the intuitive "nudges" you experience throughout your day:

- Go for a walk and see if you can focus in on your body's intuitive desire to take one route rather than another. Pay attention to what you see along this route.

- See if your intuition guides you to take a different route to work, school, the grocery store, etc.

- When it's time for a meal, take a few minutes to focus on your body. See if you can feel what your body wants in that moment, rather than what your mind is saying you "should" eat.

- In the morning, choose a favorite book and open it to a random page. Read a few sentences and see if they inform any part of your day as you move through your routine.

- Create some intuitive art using crayons and paper. Put down lines and color as you feel guided to do so, ignoring any judgments that arise from the mind as you do so.

- Whenever you are faced with a relatively minor choice (which shirt to wear, for instance), take a minute to see if you feel drawn to a specific item and go with that feeling.

EXERCISE: CONNECTING WITH AIR

Here are a couple of smaller exercises that can facilitate your connection to the clarity and vision of air:

Breath work. There are a number of different methods for working with your breath. If you are already familiar with one of these, continue to practice it. If you are new to breath work, try taking just a few minutes to close your eyes and focus on your breath. Sit silently and count to 3 or 4. Inhale slowly, hold your breath gently for 3 or 4 counts, then slowly exhale. Your breath is one of the most powerful ways you can work to feel the presence of the nagual in your physical body.

Fresh air. Stagnant air can actually affect you in a number of negative ways. You may get cranky or feel sad and not really be able to point to why. Well—let in some fresh air! Open your windows on a beautiful day and let the wind gust through your home, clearing out old energies and bringing clarity of vision. Alternatively, head for higher ground. Standing at the top of a hill after an invigorating climb, breathing in the fresh air, and looking out over the landscape can give you a great sense of refreshment and perspective.

Chapter 7

The Plaza of Fire

Fire is essential to human existence. Developing the ability to make fire at will kept our ancestors alive and healthy in cold climates and seasons. Today, we harness fire in the form of electricity, upon which we depend for so much of our daily lives that often we forget its importance—until the power goes out. And even in our modern and plugged-in lives, many of us still feel the instinctive pull to sit around an open fire at night—a cozy, wild, beautiful awe.

Yet we also know that fire is an incredibly powerful and destructive force, capable of leveling thousands of acres of forest and depriving us of our homes and sometimes our lives. Each time we strike a match or light even the smallest candle, this awesome force is present, holding the potential for both life and death. And so we work to strike a balance with fire in our day-to-day lives. We need fire and the warmth and life it provides, but we must be vigilant to keep it from burning unchecked.

In the Toltec tradition, fire represents desire and passion in all their manifestations. Fire invites us to understand that we are one with life, with the nagual itself. Fire is, in short, an expression of being joyfully and brilliantly alive. But just as with physical fire, we must work to hold this potent force within us in critical balance. We need to honor our desires and passions while tempering them with the discipline required so they don't become a raging inferno of obsession. The Toltec Warrior applies the skills of self-awareness and balance to walk this middle path.

There is a common stereotype that portrays spiritual masters and "enlightened" people as having transcended all desire. It describes them as spending the remainder of their lives sitting in serene, unmoving, silent bliss somewhere—probably on a mountain peak! But this is not the case at all. Some *are* quiet, but others may be loud, boisterous, and flamboyant. They may break into spontaneous wild dancing or fill a room with their unrestrained laughter. Both types have achieved spiritual mastery. But these masters have not lost all desires. The key is that in both instances, *their desires no longer control or define them.*

As you step into the Plaza of Fire, you do so with the understanding that passion, desire, and obsession are not light subjects. But when you learn to treat the fire within you with awareness and respect, you achieve, not only mastery over this critical aspect of your daily life, but also the ability to burn away anything in your life that no longer serves you.

Passion and Desire

While some spiritual traditions teach that desire is a bad thing (particularly with respect to sexuality), the Toltec tradition recognizes that desire is fundamentally good, because nothing in the world would happen without it. In fact, in Toltec cosmology, it was the desire of the nagual that created the whole world.

It is important to understand how important desire really is. When Toltecs say that it was the desire of the nagual that created the whole world, they mean that the basic energy of life—that life itself—*is* desire. On a purely biological level, of course, this is undeniably true. The continuation of our species would be impossible without desire. But beyond that, desire is the spark that motivates all movement, all innovation, all creation; without it, there would be only stagnation.

Fire and passion and creativity are all inextricably tied together. In fact, creativity itself would not exist without desire. Desire and passion lie at the root of every work of art that has ever moved you. Every piece of music, every breathtaking novel, every moment when an amazing achievement made your heart leap—they all began in desire.

Desire drives every new seedling that reaches upward through the soil toward the nourishment of rain and sunlight. It inspires every medical breakthrough. It moves every whale to leap up out of the sea and into the air. It causes communities to thrive and encourages the thrill of new relationships. This incredible driving force in fact influences every aspect of our lives.

For instance, do you know what activities make your heart sing? When, where, and with whom do you feel the happiest? What calls you? What thrills you? This is an opportunity for you to find out and claim what brings this sense of authentic, unrestrained joy to your life. Are you doing these things regularly? If not, why not? How can you rearrange your life in a way that feeds your passions and desires?

Of course, desire can become distorted when it is bound to the Island of Safety—your little identity. When this happens, you become attached to a desire in a way that is more about feeding your ego than about joyful wanting. This is often the case when your desires are linked to social status and material possessions. But, just as you must balance your awareness of how easily fire may burn you if mishandled with an appreciation of the critical necessity and utter beauty of fire, you must also learn to relish and appreciate the sheer joy and wonder that a balanced approach to desire can bring to your life.

Sexuality

It's also crucial to acknowledge and explore the dimension of desire and passion that includes sexuality. Many of us have grown up with a variety of domestications and limiting beliefs around sexuality, and despite decades of books and powerful movements that aim to uncover and restore a healthy approach to this aspect of our lives (and there has been a lot of progress toward that goal), it still remains a difficult topic for many. Certainly there are cultural and religious traditions that still teach that enjoying sex is sinful and unenlightened behavior. And ironically, this aversion is also reflected in some contemporary spiritual and/or self-help movements. In this latter case, all sense of sexual desire is either glossed over in favor of generalities or else perceived as being associated with the body and therefore something that must be transcended in favor of the mind, soul, or spirit.

This is not the Toltec way. Our tradition sees healthy sexuality as a near-direct physical expression of the nagual—of life force and creativity. When the fire of sexuality is balanced, it is beautiful, life-affirming, and a great gift. But most of us have grown up with an ingrained reluctance to talk about sexuality. This reluctance is buried deep within almost all of us, and it takes time to move through it. But it's important to learn to talk about sexuality and examine our domestications surrounding it in order to craft a future sex life free of guilt and shame. Only then can we achieve true personal freedom. Our goal is to approach sexuality with a sense of curiosity, joy, presence, and detachment, lest we fall into the trap of punishing ourselves for wrestling with these issues at all.

There are two ways to explore this part of our work. The first relates sex to the act of lovemaking; the second relates sex to biology and gender—for instance, our beliefs and domestications around what it means to "be a man," or "be a woman," or other gender expressions beyond the binary.

Many people, perhaps most, create part of their identity around their sexuality or some aspect of it (and this includes asexuality and celibacy as well). Remember:

This is neither right or wrong. It's just the current situation in the Dream of the Planet. The work in the Plaza of Fire, as in each plaza you explore, is to apply your skills of awareness to your inner life and try to notice when and where you are attaching yourself to these identities and where they may be causing suffering in your life. Are you holding on to old ideas and beliefs that require further investigation? Do some of your beliefs, assumptions, and domestications need to be changed or released? Here are some questions that may help uncover underlying domestications that relate to sexuality:

- *Am I able to speak freely with my partner(s) about sex? If not, why not?*

- *Do I place part of my sense of self in my sexual prowess—my level of experience and/or the number of partners I've had?* In our culture, this is especially common in men, but it certainly occurs with women as well, often in the opposite fashion.

- *Do I sometimes use sex as a tool to get what I want?* This is neither inherently positive or negative behavior, unless you are deceptive about it. If you do, what consequences might this have for your relationships, if any?

This is work in which your journal may be especially helpful, as it provides a private place where you can be free and safe to explore your thoughts and feelings around these questions fully. If you feel comfortable, however, you may also find it fruitful to engage your partner in an exploratory conversation. Ultimately, the goal is to craft a sex life for yourself that is passionate, consensual, free of guilt and shame, engaged in open awareness, and cleared of any old beliefs and domestications. The soul of intimacy blossoms when we heal the wounds that brought fear, guilt, and judgment of our own sensuality. To enjoy our sexuality is to be free to feel and enjoy our sensuality.

It is also important to consider your ideas surrounding what it means to be a person of your gender. Different cultures treat gender in different ways. Here are some questions you can ask yourself to explore this topic:

- *What does it mean to me to be a man or a woman?*

- *What are some of the ways in which my own beliefs and domestications around gender influence my behavior?*

- *Are there ways in which some of these domestications have been limiting me?*

• *Has my biological sex or gender expression become attached to the identity I've created for myself?*

This last question can be tricky, as associations with biological sex and gender expression are sometimes so ingrained that it is difficult to see exactly where they become part of your identity, or even how the Dream of the Planet has influenced your ideas about them.

A perfect example of this lies in the "traditional" gender colors—pink for girls; blue for boys. These colors were originally seen in a completely opposite way. In the early 1900s, pink was considered the "stronger" color, and so was appropriate for boys. Blue was considered the "daintier" color, and so was appropriate for girls. Over time, for various reasons, the color associations were switched. And now, these arbitrary assignments have become so much a part of our understanding of what it means to be male or female that a man may grow up feeling that wearing a pink shirt isn't "manly."

This clearly shows how the beliefs, thoughts, preferences, and ideas that are a part of the Dream of the Planet are all based on our agreements, and nothing more. And of course, these ingrained gender agreements reach out into many other aspects of our lives that are far more profound, influencing us all in areas of career, division of labor at home, self-confidence, skill-building, etc.

Obsession

When passion and desire move from a well-tended fire to a raging inferno, that's when we encounter the truly negative consequence of desire—obsession.

Obsession is an expression of conditional love. When obsession drives you and bends your desire and passion in a destructive direction, you may make negative self-judgments that then influence your actions. *If I don't get this job, I am a failure. This is my only chance for happiness. If I'm not married by the time I'm thirty-five, I'll be alone forever and it will prove that I'm unlovable.* These and many other deeply held ultimatums can twist your desires and dreams into conditions under which you must succeed at all costs. And this is not freedom.

I mentioned earlier in the book how comparison and competition can fuel the inferno of obsession. For this reason, becoming aware of your tendency to compare and compete with others can help you uncover instances in which your authentic passion and desire have become warped. In the current Dream of the Planet, comparison and competition are often seen as forces that help push us forward, but this is true only in the short run. In the long run, they're much more likely to lead to more self-judgment or to box you into a false sense of identity—the "I" of your domesticated self. As your reliance on your little identity grows stronger due to comparison and competition, you are likely to resent the success of others, as though life were a zero-sum game. You are also likely to reject yourself when you miss the mark.

Try to notice all the little ways in which you compete with others, whether it be at work, in your family, or in social circles. Become aware of the comparisons you make concerning material possessions, income, or physical attributes. This is a mental habit for most of us. But when you operate from this perspective, you ultimately create more suffering for yourself, because it's a game you can never really win. When you play it, you lose your clarity and your sense of oneness—within yourself and with others, with all living things, and with the universe itself.

The key to changing this habitual behavior begins with noticing when your mind indulges in it, and then bringing unconditional love to the situation instead. When you simply drop the compare-and-compete narrative by recognizing it, acknowledging it, and bringing love to yourself and others, you begin the transformation process and remember that we are all part of the nagual.

I can tell you from experience that it is very possible to pursue your dreams and passions with *unconditional* love as the motivating force. When this happens, you enjoy the pursuit of a dream, as well as the achievement of that dream. You also appreciate and accept the movement of life even if the dream is never achieved. The free expression of desire that is grounded in unconditional love allows you to celebrate the success of others as much as your own. Toltec Warriors keep their focus on the inner self and know that they get what they need, all the time—and that others get what they need, all the time.

To be clear, this doesn't mean that you shouldn't enjoy situations where competition is used for fun, as in games or sports. I, for one, am very passionate when I play and watch sports, and the competition definitely adds an element of excitement. The difference is that, when the game or event is over, *the competition in my mind ends as well.* I am careful not to take the results of the game and make them a condition of my happiness and self-acceptance.

The key in the Plaza of Fire is to learn the art of balance. When you have a passion for something, a big yearning for it, ask yourself if it is something that primarily feeds your little self, your ego. Or is it something that brings you joy? Sometimes the answer will be both. When this is the case, remember to focus on the joy.

The Gift of Destruction

We all know that fire can destroy—whether it consumes a few cedar branches in a campfire or several thousand acres of wilderness. But it is also true that destruction itself is a natural and necessary part of life.

For indigenous cultures of the Americas, fire has long been an important part of ceremonial life, as well as a means to maintain the natural landscape. Controlled burning of vegetation at certain times of the year or in multiyear cycles was and is central to our stewardship of the land. It perpetuates the natural food chain and helps to maintain essential ecosystems. By contrast, many land management practices today forbid any kind of burning. Forestry services are just beginning to rethink this, however, particularly after several seasons of devastating wildfires in the West. From a scientific standpoint, there's quite a lot of evidence to support the practice of controlled burns. They clear out brush, diseased plants, and pests; they return important minerals to the soil; and they create new space in which young plants can access sunlight and water. Plus, there are some trees that only reproduce with the help of fire, like the giant sequoias.

You can cultivate a reverence for this kind of destruction as well, particularly for the ways in which it prepares the landscape of your life for rebirth. Of course, I recognize that this is more easily said than done, particularly as you weather the initial stormy chaos of things falling apart—such as when you lose a job or a relationship falls apart. Nonetheless, you can gain a kind of perspective on destruction from these experiences that can offer you some solace and show you a way to move forward.

For example, many years ago, I experienced a particularly profound moment of clarity in the wake of a difficult breakup. The breakup itself was so painful that it made me afraid in some ways to become romantically involved again. This is a common response to pain, and unfortunately, we can't rush the healing process, even if it hurts a lot. We have to move through the pain and allow it to move through us. This can be a kind of "releasing into the fire" moment. But, as I discovered, when we give ourselves the permission and the time to allow the burning rush of emotion to run its course, it is often closely followed by a period of deep healing.

After such a powerful experience, our lives may not return to "normal." But once we are on the other side, we often find that we wouldn't have wanted them to. Many of these painful processes help us move forward into the next chapter of our lives. In the case of my breakup, for example, I learned lessons about myself that helped me become the person with whom my wife eventually fell in love.

You face your fears after a heartbreak or a loss of love by becoming even more aware that *you are the source of love*. It doesn't come from outside of you. Once you remove fear from the equation, you accept the fact that sometimes people leave us and that's okay. You can let the destruction be what it is and not try to control it. It's okay to feel heartbreak and to feel the pain of losing someone. And you don't have to make new flawed agreements driven by a fear of getting hurt again.

The key is to embrace the idea of allowing the element of fire to burn away what you no longer need, and to do it consciously. What do you need to burn away from your life in order to make room for new growth? I invite you to take a moment right now and identify a single item or belief that you have used to bolster your false identity and allow the metaphorical fire of unconditional love to burn it away, leaving you free and clear to embrace new opportunities and ideas.

Fire is a dynamic and complex element. It is two things at once at all times—creativity and destruction. Thus the lessons it offers are also dynamic and complex. But when you approach fire with awareness and attention to balance, you find that life blooms, opening out like a magnificent flower fueled by its natural desire to embrace joy in the warmth of sunlight.

EXERCISE: IGNITING THE SPARK OF LIFE

The nagual moves through all the elements and through all living things. But sometimes it is easiest to visualize in terms of fire—as a radiant light or energy moving through your cells, or crackling raw electricity, or a dynamic, roiling ball of flame and heat in the center of the earth, waiting for you to tap into it and turn it into the creative masterpiece that is your life. Through the metaphor of fire, you can feel the nagual's motivating energy calling you to say yes to life, to dance and sing and move with exhilaration and enthusiasm. And beyond the metaphorical, you can also learn to sense this energy with your body by tuning in to the nagual in the heart of the natural world.

For this exercise, find a spot outside where you can be comfortable and relatively uninterrupted for a length of time. If you can be in physical contact with an element of nature, all the better—sit with your back to a tree, or on a large boulder, or with your bare feet in the grass. Settle into the space and take a few deep breaths. Let go of any worries or anxieties that may be keeping you from the present moment. Lengthen your spine and let your head rest gently atop it, so that you feel relaxed but supported in as upright a position as possible.

Now imagine that you are a connecting circuit, a conduit between the fire in the sky and the fire in the heart of the earth. Imagine a ray of energy from the sun coming down through your head and spine and traveling deep into the heart of the earth. Here, it taps into the ball of light, heat, and energy in the center of the planet, merges with it, and returns back up into your body through the base of your spine, up into your head, and out into the sky. This energy is constantly moving—from the sky down into the earth and back up—in a never-ceasing dance of light and movement and pure life.

Allow this energy to move out to infuse your whole body and clear out any shadowy patches or stagnant energy. Feel encased in a warm egg of vibrant, healing, golden light. There is nothing that separates you from this energy. It exists at all times in your body and the bodies of the sun and the earth. It's just that you are only now noticing it and acknowledging it. You may even feel a light tingling or warmth on your skin as your body welcomes this influx of refreshing life-force energy.

Stay quiet for a few minutes. You don't need to "do" anything. Just feel the energy move and sense your connection to the earth.

When you're ready to stop the exercise, imagine the ball of light that surrounds you getting smaller, until it is a tiny radiant glow in your solar plexus. It leaves behind it a fully nourished well of energy within each cell of your body, which is then gently released back out into the sky and/or down into the earth. Take a few more deep breaths, open your eyes, and stretch. If you feel over-energized—as if you've had one too many cups of coffee—you can "ground" the excess energy by placing your hands directly on the earth and imagining any energy you don't immediately need draining out and down into the earth, where it will be recycled back into its work of nourishing and enlivening every living thing.

Know that, even though you've released your circuit of energy back out into the world, the nagual is still flowing through you and that, through this exercise, any places in your mind, heart, or body that were in need of refreshment have been filled again with this rich energy.

If this is the first time you've ever done an exercise like this, don't be discouraged if you don't feel anything physical or if you find the visualization challenging. The nagual is always there—it is you, whether you perceive it directly or not. And, as with other exercises in this book, you will benefit from repeating this one over time.

When you have finished the exercise, pay attention to your energy levels for the rest of the day. See if you notice any differences in how you approach various projects. Do you feel excited about something new or refreshed regarding an old project? This is also a good time to take stock of any goals, dreams, and other desires you've had percolating in the back of your mind, but that you may have dismissed as unrealistic or unobtainable. Look at some of these with fresh eyes and see if there may be something new in them you haven't seen before.

EXERCISE: CULTIVATING SYMPATHETIC JOY

We talked in this chapter about how comparison and competition can change the pursuit of joy into an ego-building obsession. This exercise can help you stay focused on the joy rather than the ego. It is based on a Buddhist practice appropriately named "sympathetic joy," in which you cultivate a conscious sense of happiness and gratitude for other people's success, wellness, and advancement.

As with so many other aspects of mastery, it begins with personal awareness. If you find yourself in a situation where someone else has achieved or received something that you think you want for yourself—a material object, a job, a relationship, or some sort of social recognition— the first thing you will likely notice is that jealousy or envy arises inside you. When this occurs, try to determine the origin of these feelings. Where do these emotions come from? Is there a story you tell yourself around this issue? Notice any ideas of comparison and competition around the situation. Then consider if and how you have formed an identity around these ideas. The stronger the feeling of envy or jealousy, the greater the degree to which you have tied your identity to it.

Now take a breath and consciously remind yourself that you and the other person are both part of the nagual, and that we all get exactly what we need, all the time. There are no exceptions to this. Finally, send the person involved intentions of congratulations and well-wishes in your own mind. In other words, mentally celebrate the person's success. This can be extremely difficult in some situations, and you may even feel as if you are faking it. And that's okay, you are just breaking an old agreeement that no longer serves you.

As with other practices in this book, I hope you repeat this one often and see how you feel afterward. Soon, you will likely find that your feelings of envy and jealousy lessen. And you may even end up being genuinely happy for the other person. The other benefit to this practice is that, when you achieve something that someone else wants, your identity with that lessens as well. You will find that you no longer feel superior to others. Your perception becomes clear, because the truth is that we all get what we need, all the time. We are all part of the nagual.

EXERCISE: CONNECTING WITH FIRE

Here are a couple of smaller exercises that can facilitate your connection to the passion and energy of fire:

Sacred fire. Fire focuses human attention very quickly in a spirit of reverence and awe. That's why it's an especially powerful element in ritual practices. Even the simple act of lighting a candle before journaling or meditation can send a potent signal to your mind that something sacred is underway. The sound of a match being struck, the flare of light and heat, are wonderful symbols for new beginnings. On a larger scale, there is something ancient and exhilarating about singing, dancing, or even just sitting and contemplating around an open fire.

Cleansing fire. As discussed earlier in the chapter, fire is also a rich symbol for the shedding of the old in exchange for the new. To that end, consider performing a small ceremony wherein you write down a few items you'd like to release on strips of paper and burn them in a fireplace, firepit, or even a fireproof bowl. The family of a friend of mine performs a ceremony like this every New Year's Eve to mark the passing of the old year and embrace the potential of the new. One year when they didn't have access to a fireplace, they bought some flash paper from a shop that sells stage magic props and burned it over candles, which added mystery, beauty, and drama to an already powerful family ritual.

Chapter 8

The Plaza of Earth

A priest walked into a pub, indignant to find so many of his parishioners there. He rounded them up and shepherded them into the church. Then he solemnly said: "All those who want to go to heaven, step over here to the left." Everyone stepped over except one man, who stubbornly stood his ground.

The priest looked at him fiercely and said: "Don't you want to go to heaven?"

"No," said the man.

"Do you mean to stand there and tell me you don't want to go to heaven when you die?"

The man looked puzzled. "Of course I want to go to heaven when I die. I just thought you were going right now!"

This humorous little story from Anthony de Mello provides an appropriate introduction to the next stop on your journey, the Plaza of Earth.

From time immemorial, the earth has been a symbol of our physical bodies. This is only natural, because our bodies are, in fact, a part of the earth. The food we eat, the air we breathe, and the water we drink are all part of the great cycles of the living planet. Moreover, our story-telling minds easily make symbolic connections between the bones and muscles of our bodies and the ground and rocks beneath our feet.

In the Toltec tradition, all physical matter is called the *tonal*. This includes our bodies, the land, and all we can engage with our physical senses. Yet even though it is beautiful and miraculous, ultimately the tonal is life-less without the nagual, bereft of the energetic, moving fire of being. We may recognize this intuitively, yet the vast majority of us still mistake our physical bodies for our true being. We take the tonal to *be* the nagual, and as a result, we fear that when our bodies die, that it is the end of us as well. Mistaking our bodies for who we really are is perhaps the ultimate source of all our fears. Moving beyond this into a deep understanding of what and who you really are is thus one of the last hurdles you face in the mastery of life.

I personally encountered this reality many years ago, when I was at my uncle's bedside when he passed away. I was holding his hand when he was declared brain dead due to the swelling in his brain. But even after that, I could still feel his presence. His hand was warm and alive. I felt him, even though they told me he was gone. Then, in a moment, I could no longer feel him. His warmth disappeared, and I went from holding the hand of a living being to holding an inanimate object. I knew at that moment that the nagual had left his body.

Being present for my uncle's death taught me one of the biggest lessons of my life: I am not my body. I think I believed this mentally to some degree before this experience, but at that moment, when I felt it happen skin to skin, I knew in my bones that we are something more than our physical flesh and blood. Experience replaced belief.

When I tell this story to groups, I often say that the body is dead the moment it's conceived. I know this can seem confusing, so I want to be clear. I say this to underscore the point that our bodies only move because the nagual moves them. All beings that live and breathe are part of and expressions of the nagual—you and me and every living person on earth this very minute. Without this vital essence (our true selves), everything is just tonal. The body is not life; we *give* it life.

Avenue of the Dead

On our journey through Teotihuacan, we have been walking down the Avenue of the Dead, and my guess is that you have now figured out the mystical meaning of that name. Although the Aztecs named it as such because they mistakenly believed that the avenue was lined with tombs of past kings, the Avenue of the Dead actually serves as a potent reminder to us that our bodies move one step closer to death with every passing moment; everything that is born must die. This is not meant to be a morbid or pessimistic proclamation. In fact, it's just the opposite. When we truly realize that our bodies will inevitably die and that we are closer to death now than we have ever been, it serves as a potent reminder for us to focus on being truly alive.

In the Toltec tradition, we often talk about the angel of death—a shadow who walks with each of us at all times and in all situations. Again, this is not meant to be scary or threatening. It is simply a reminder that our bodies, as well as all our physical possessions, are *on loan.* We never truly own these physical things. And you can use this awareness of death to deepen your mindfulness of the present moment and increase your happiness. For instance, what would you be doing today if you knew that tomorrow the angel of death would come for you? The master answers that question instantly and honestly: I would do exactly what I am doing right now. Masters live each day in utter awareness that it may be their last, yet are also aware that today we are the youngest we will ever be.

This doesn't mean that they have achieved some kind of impossibly perfect life wherein every moment is free of pain or difficult experiences. Rather it means that, in their achievement of personal freedom and in their acceptance of the impermanence of their physical lives, they are able to accept each moment as it is on its own terms—and then let it go. The idea of death walks with the Toltec Warrior as a reminder that this moment, just now, is the only reality; accepting that reality without clinging to it or running from it is true freedom.

The Toltecs are not alone in this practice. For instance, the people who live in Bhutan, who are known for their joyfulness, follow a spiritual practice that directs them to think about death five times a day. By refusing to run from the prospect of their inevitable death and instead spending conscious time daily pondering it, the Bhutanese embrace the uncertainty of life, accept the imperfect perfection of the present moment, and release their attachments. They know that bodily death is an inextricable part of life.

Fear of Living

The fear of death is incredibly powerful and pervasive. Examples can be found all over the world in various cultures and periods of history that attest to the human desire to live forever and escape death. But I suggest that, even greater than our fear of dying, is our fear of truly living. I believe that we are deeply afraid of the great unknown, of all the potential errors and mistakes we may make (and the punishing voice of the parasite insisting that we will always fail).

This great terror of uncertainty makes it difficult for us to talk openly about death. Just as with sexuality, our culture has domesticated us into silence on this issue. The underlying agreement seems to be that, if we never speak of dying or make any plans or have any conversations with our families and friends about it, then somehow, magically, it will never happen. But of course, we all have experienced, or eventually will, the loss of a loved one. And we will all eventually die ourselves. Death, then, is both a potent reminder that the tonal is impermanent and a beautifully crafted invitation to use your time here wisely, to not take it for granted. Starting now, in this very moment, you can be the artist of your life and paint your masterpiece. There is no need to wait. In this moment, you are alive.

Moreover, while what we understand to be physical death is something we all must one day experience, at a deeper level, death is merely a scary story created by the human mind. Don't get me wrong: it's natural to feel grief and sadness over losing a loved one. But Toltec Warriors recognize that, in death, it is truly only the tonal, the physical body, that reaches an ending. The energy, the essence, the nagual continues on into eternity. When we fully accept this reality, we begin to heal. Our culture presents life and death as opposites, but the truth is that *birth* and death are the true opposites, holding between them the physical existence of the tonal. Life itself, the radiant nagual, *has no opposite*.

While the Toltec tradition has been teaching this for generations, modern science has also proven that energy itself cannot be created or destroyed, only transformed. The same is true for water, which is part of the energy of life. There has never been any more or less water on the planet than there is right now. It simply changes from gas to liquid to solid in a never-ending cycle. So the energy that animates the body does not "die." Rather it is transformed into something else. *Life* continues, always. This is another reason why we work so diligently to become aware of the illusory nature of our small selves, our ego identities—because they are inextricably tied to the same fundamental error that causes us to cling to the body, or the tonal.

The Gift of the Body

While the Toltec tradition teaches that the tonal is not who we are, it also teaches that the body is a great gift to be treasured. For this reason, it's important to look at our domesticated ideas about our physical selves.

We judge our bodies. We reject them or wish they were different in some way. Or perhaps we neglect or punish them in the name of progress and perfection. Virtually everyone on the planet suffers from this error in some way. But here at the Plaza of Earth, you can come into a whole new relationship with your body by realizing that it is your gift for this lifetime. On this part of your journey, you learn to enter into the sacred care, and release, of your own body.

The human body is a miracle. It has its own intelligence that operates well outside of the human mind. Without any input from the conscious, thinking mind, our bodies take in life-giving oxygen, pump this oxygen throughout themselves using a vast and complex network, digest food, heal cuts and bruises and scrapes, and carry out countless other critical functions, all on their own. They employ remarkable processing centers—eyes, ears, tongue, skin, nose—to receive light, sound, texture, taste, and scent. Information from these centers helps us navigate the world, as well as perceive and simply enjoy the delights of food, dance, art, and music.

But each body is different. We all need different combinations of sleep, healthy foods, sunlight, and exercise. We are tempted by different harmful substances. By remaining aware of your physical state, you can open up a direct line of communication with your own body's wisdom. Your existing agreements about the body can really blur these lines of communication within you. But you can turn these agreements into conditions of self-acceptance. You can learn to hold them in curiosity, exploration, and ever-shifting balance instead.

Today, the Dream of the Planet is plagued by an almost relentless sense of busyness. Many now feel as if they can barely get through each day, with its seemingly endless list of tasks and not enough time to do them all. The result is that our levels of stress are consistently high, and that affects us physically as well as emotionally and mentally. But how this busyness manifests—where the balance lies between being joyfully engaged and stressfully overstimulated—is different for each individual.

We all have different domestications and beliefs surrounding issues of work, laziness, and worth, and we all have different ways in which we achieve rest and balance. Moreover, we have to make sure that we don't turn our need for balance into yet another condition or agreement. *I am terrible at taking care of myself. I am so lazy and can't seem to get through a single day without a nap.* So it becomes important to approach this with real awareness and openness until you find what's best for you.

For instance, you may have a craving for a salty snack, and then beat yourself up about always eating the "wrong" things. And yet, if you go still, take some deep breaths, and tune in to that craving with acceptance and love, you may find out something important. You may be dehydrated. And your body knows that, when you eat something salty, you are likely to seek out hydration immediately afterward. Or you may be low on sodium, which is essential for proper bodily functioning. Or your body may simply be asking you to slow down and treat it to something you enjoy. All of these are valid scenarios; only you can pinpoint what is true for you.

One way to do this is to pause throughout your day and ask yourself what your body needs *right now*. Does it need rest? Or movement? Or sunlight? We often ignore the subtler signals our bodies send us and only pay attention to them when they become a desperate scream. The key is to listen in and open the lines of communication before things get to that point.

Take some time to explore what pleasure feels like in your physical body. I don't only mean sensual or sexual pleasure—although, as we found in the previous chapter, that's important too. Some of us have been domesticated to look down on all bodily pleasures, even in their simplest forms. In fact, the withholding of pleasure is a powerful tool of control in the Dream of the Planet.

Because of this, it may be helpful to start with small simple acts that bring pleasure to your body. For example, sitting in the sun. Or putting your bare feet into cool water. Or taking a long relaxing warm bath. Or adding plants and fresh flowers to your home. Or wearing clothing that feels good on your body. Or taking a nap. If you encounter any negative reactions—if you find yourself thinking that these things are selfish or a waste of time, or that you don't deserve them, or that you should be doing something for someone else, or that first you have to finish every single thing on your to-do list—investigate these reactions. You may find some unexposed domestications around the idea of pleasure or self-care.

When you feel exhausted by life, it can indicate that you've been tricked by your inner parasite. Whenever you push yourself to do more or achieve more in an effort to *be* more, it means you believe that you aren't enough as you are. The Plaza of Earth reminds you to honor your body's needs. Rest when you need to rest; eat when you need to eat; move when you need to move. Don't push your body to do more out of fear and/or anxiety. If your basic needs in life are met and you still have an identity built around endless exhaustion, ask yourself why you are saying yes to fatigue. What's in it for the little you?

Bodies of Light

The Toltec tradition teaches that the magnificent human body, this great gift, is made of light and stars. My father, don Miguel Ruiz, in his book *The Four Agreements*, recounts the story of the ancient shaman who looks up at the night sky and realizes: *I am made of light. I am made of stars.*

As it turns out, modern science now agrees. Recently, astrophysicists have explained how the elements of the periodic table that make up the building blocks of our physical bodies originated in stars that went supernova millions of years ago. So our bodies really *are* made of stars. As for light, while most people know that nothing on this planet would exist without the light of the sun, scientists have also discovered that the human body actually *emits* light at a level that can't be seen with the naked eye.

So the truth is that our miraculous bodies are part of the starry cosmos just as much as they are of the planet. Hence the Dream of the Planet has become the Dream of the Universe. Our physical connection to the stars is yet another reason why we say in the Toltec tradition that there need not be any separation between heaven and earth. You can create heaven on earth right now by realizing that you are the nagual and using the gift of your body to help create your masterpiece.

Mirror of Truth

An old story tells how, long ago, Truth existed high above us in the heavens in the form of a single mirror. One day, this mirror broke and fell to earth in shards. Some people picked up a single shard and proclaimed it was the truth; others gathered as many shards as they could and tried to piece them together into a different truth. Of course, deciding that one or even a few shards are the same as the whole truth seems foolish, and yet that's what most of us do.

The one exception to this, however, may be the historical and cultural figures we know as tricksters or fools. In many traditions, fools are holy. They are closer than most of us to accessing the whole truth, because, instead of trying to cling to a single shard of the mirror, they have their feet firmly planted in the land of not-knowing, on the street of upside down, in the house of saying-things-that-others-don't-want-to-hear. They move through rooms of joy, uncertainty, and paradox—all of which reflect a version of that mirror of truth that is more than any of the single shards can show. Fools and tricksters have important messages for us, but they don't care if we listen or not. They know that they are just as likely to be wrong as we are. They reflect us back to ourselves, sometimes in our most ridiculous or pitiful moments. They are master shape-shifters and manipulators of perspective; they show us a world turned upside down.

The Toltecs also told of a great mirror of truth that exists in the Plaza of Earth. Imagine for a moment that you are in the Plaza of Earth in the middle of the night after several days of rain. The skies have cleared, but the plaza itself has been flooded and is now a vast, still, soft puddle. The stars hang above in an inky black sky. This is the place where you remember your physical body and honor it as a gift. It's where you understand that your life on earth is a gift from death and that it can be taken away at any time. And yet the Plaza of Earth offers you one more profound insight before you go.

You walk into the shallow puddle and let the waters return to stillness around you. You look down at your feet, at the earth, your home. But instead of seeing the rocks and dirt that you are accustomed to seeing there, you see the stars. Galaxies at your feet. The world turned upside down. You are walking in the stars, standing in a mirror of the universe, and you realize: *Yes, of course.* You are at home in your body, with your feet on the ground, as a child of Mother Earth. But you are also of the stars; you are also a body of light. You were never just material, just tonal. You are, and always have been, nagual.

EXERCISE: DEATH
VISUALIZATION AND MEDITATION

As you begin this exercise, I want to be clear that it is not intended to make you dwell on depressing or dark themes. Its goal is to cultivate your unconditional love for the present moment and for the gift of your body. The truth is that, the more you confront your fears about death, the freer you become.

In this exercise, you will visualize your own funeral. I suggest images of your culture's final rites symbols, perhaps flowers or a church setting. In my own case, I see the marigold flower, as that has come to be a symbol of what constitutes a funeral and the Day of the Dead celebrations in our culture. If you want to use different images to make your visualization more unique and authentic to you, please do not hesitate to do so.

To begin, find a place where you can sit comfortably and be uninterrupted for approximately twenty minutes. Settle into a sitting position that is comfortable, but not so relaxed that you risk falling asleep. Some like to lie down for this meditation so they can visualize their own death in a more physical way. If you choose to do this, however, try to do your meditation earlier in the day so you will be less inclined to doze off.

Allow yourself to become as relaxed as possible. Take several slow, deep breaths, and imagine a wave of warm, golden light moving slowly from the top of your head down to your feet and toes, relaxing each part of your body as it moves through you. If you notice any anxieties in your mind or tensions in your body, spend some time acknowledging them and letting them go. Allow them to move through and beyond you, like clouds passing over a mountain.

Now picture in your mind's eye your own funeral or memorial service—outside at a local park or wilderness area, at a place of worship, or in your home. Imagine a place that feels right to you. It can help to choose a real place, one that you have been to before and can picture easily.

Imagine that you are floating slightly above this place, as you are now an aware presence without any physical form. Begin to notice people arriving—loved ones, friends, and family. They are all gathering around a table that has been set up as a memorial space. The table holds photos of you throughout your life, bouquets of beautiful flowers, and a casket containing your body—your tonal. The casket is open. Imagine seeing your body lying in the casket after your life force, the nagual, has left it.

When you look at the others present, you can see that they are made of a radiant light. When you look around, you notice that this light is reflected in every living thing around you—the bark of trees, the blades of grass, everything. You can now see that all living things are part of this intense, incredible light, but that the people in attendance do not know this. You realize that you are also a being of pure light and that you have always been so. You feel a wave of enormous love and gratitude well up within you.

As your friends and loved ones comfort each other, spend some time with each of them and bless them. Let the love and gratitude you feel for your life on earth spill out and over everyone, up and out into the sky and among the trees. Your death is only the end for your physical body, which will return to the earth. This shining body of light that remains behind lives forever. As you realize this, allow the light to grow stronger and brighter, moving out and merging with the light emanating from every other living thing. Say these words aloud or in your mind, and feel the truth of them: "I was never born. I can never die. I am not my physical body. I am the nagual."

Stay in this meditation for the next few minutes, repeating that mantra as many times as you like. When you feel the meditation has come to its natural end, slowly become aware of your body. Move your fingers and toes, your hands and feet, your arms and legs. Slowly open your eyes. You are still nagual, but you are also alive in a living body, a part of the earth. There will come a day when your physical body will die, but *you* will never die.

EXERCISE: LISTENING TO YOUR BODY

Today, there are very few who are able to say that they love every part of their physical bodies completely and unashamedly. We are so inundated with domestications and agreements that make us see some part of our bodies, or even our entire bodies, as somehow inferior. Our bodies never seem to be "enough"—attractive enough, athletic enough, young enough, energetic enough, tall enough, thin enough. As a result, we often stop paying attention to their legitimate needs and focus instead on what we believe and agree they "should" need. *I should be twenty pounds lighter. I should have darker hair. I should run five miles a day.* This exercise can help you really listen to your body and learn its true needs.

In your journal, spend some time considering your relationship to your body in light of everything you've learned in the Plaza of Earth. This is a difficult topic that can prompt deep emotional reactions, so approach this time with compassion, forgiveness, and gentleness. Go slowly, and be watchful for traps wherein the mitote may try to turn an authentic need into a condition or a "should." There is a difference between your body telling you that it needs more movement and an inner voice saying you are lazy and don't work out enough.

Below are some sample questions to ask yourself two to three times a day. This is not an all-inclusive list, but questions like these can help you get into a regular practice of checking in with your physical body in a new way.

How does my body feel? Check in with your body in this moment. How does it feel? Try to state this without attaching any judgment or value to it. Are you cold? Hot? Do you have any aches and pains? Are you tired? If so, what does that mean? Are you physically tired or is it more accurate to say that you are emotionally tired or bored?

What does my body need? Ask yourself what your body needs most in this moment. Does it need to rest? A glass of water? A quick walk around the neighborhood? Again, listen carefully and try to make the distinction between what your mind and its agreements *think* your body needs and what your body is actually asking for in this moment.

EXERCISE: CONNECTING WITH EARTH

Here are a couple of smaller exercises that can help facilitate your connection to the grounding nature of earth:

Build an ancestor shrine. Death is a part of your bodily life. The more work you can do to absorb this truth and learn how to live with it without fear and in joy, the more freedom you will enjoy. Because death is not the end, your connections to your loved ones move beyond it. Therefore, it may help you to connect with the powerful, earthy realities of death by reaching out to loved ones who have passed on. You can do this by creating and maintaining an ancestor shrine. This can be elaborate—with candles, food, drink, flowers, etc—or simple—a photograph with a small votive candle in front of it. The important thing is to spend at least a few minutes with the altar on a regular basis (weekly or even daily), telling your ancestors that you love them. If possible, try to engage in some meditation and reflection on death and its role in our physical lives. Imagine that the same energy that animated their bodies is animating yours.

Explore a cave. If possible, spend some time in a cavern or cave. There may be one in your area that offers guided tours. These are incredible opportunities to sink deep beneath the surface of the world and see the wonder and beauty that is normally locked away in the secret deep places of the earth. Some tour guides may even allow you to spend a few minutes in complete darkness, which can offer profound moments of meditation and reflection. Breathe deeply and send your gratitude, wonder, and awe out to Mother Earth. This is your home. This ground beneath you, this body. You may run, drive, stomp, and cartwheel over the moss and grass and pavement all day long and never think about how much the earth supports you every second of your life. Take this moment to say thank you.

Chapter 9

The Pyramid of the Moon

The moon has long been a symbol for reflection and renewal. Because the moon renews itself every twenty-nine days in a cycle of constant rebirth, it provided a natural template for marking the passage of time in early calendar systems. Moreover, many ancient civilizations saw a symbolic link between the moon's cycle and women's reproductive cycles, a link we can see in myths and stories involving moon goddesses.

When we consider the moon's ability to move the great oceans with her gravitational pull and combine this with the fact that the majority of our own bodies are made of water, it's easy to understand how the moon has been held in such high regard by cultures around the world. And the majesty, mystery, and cyclical nature of the moon can help you understand the inherent cycles in your own life and on your spiritual journey.

As we discussed at the beginning of this book, one way to see the journey to mastery is as a deepening spiral. You return to the same lessons over and over throughout your life. But you also bring along with you all of the work you have done. You don't have to become frustrated when the same issues or the same emotional reactions surface, because you are deepening your spiral as you deal with them. Like any great spiritual practice, this journey is never "finished" or "perfect." It is a living, changing, and growing process that continues through time—like the moon.

Here at the Pyramid of the Moon, you pause to rest, to renew yourself, and to reflect on your journey thus far. Here, you begin to see the power of your journey as a physical representation of the two-headed feathered serpent god Quetzalcoatl. You began at the Plaza of Quetzalcoatl with the distorting and self-harming voices of the parasite and judge. As you passed through the plazas of the mind and of the elements, you learned how to confront and release your unhelpful agreements and limiting beliefs. Now you find yourself at the foot of the Pyramid of the Moon—an in-between space where you are no longer in your old life, but not yet in your new one. You have examined the identities you created along the way, and now you can symbolically return to the Mother, to the womb, to a place of wholeness where you existed before your fear-based domestications took over. In this sense, this step on your journey—climbing the Pyramid of the Moon—is a kind of rebirth.

Let's take a moment to review the various surrenders you have made on your journey so far. After leaving the Island of Safety, the home of your little self and seat of the identity you have always clung to, you passed through the Plaza of the Mind, where you learned to identify, investigate, and release the unhelpful domestications that live there. You began to practice the mastery of awareness—the primary tool used to heal the mind. Then you visited the Plaza of Water, where you learned to recognize your emotional states and how your parasite hijacks your emotions to keep you trapped in old stories and behaviours. You learned to harness forgiveness and release and purify your emotional body, balancing its wisdom with that of the mind. In the Plaza of Air, you committed to clear vision and embraced the truth of infinite possibility, learning to trust your intuition in your work to be the artist of your life. In the Plaza of Fire, you burned away the illusion of separation and reconnected to the passionate spirit that flows through you, creating life itself. In the Plaza of Earth, you faced the fear of death and embraced the paradox of living a life in the gift of a physical body as a singular and unique expression of the nagual.

And through all of it, you've been healing yourself.

As you reflect back on your work throughout the journey, you may realize that we are all—you, me, and everyone else—simultaneously completely unique, yet utterly the same. You are not your body, not your thoughts, not your emotions; but you *are* the nagual that created the whole thing. You are connected to me, and I to you. We are both nagual. We are the stars and the sun. We are the truth. We create everything we know, and knowledge obeys us, not the other way around. Our mind now is the ally, no longer distorting our knowledge and our perception of life.

You need no gurus, no priests, because the truth has always been inside you. This is what you've been searching for your entire life; you have simply recognized this search on your journey. You know that the Divine is within you, and you no longer have to search for it. You know that hell only exists in the mind, and only in the moment that you decide to punish or hurt yourself.

At the start of this journey, we said that Teotihuacan can be translated as "the place where humans recognize the divinity within themselves." As you leave the Avenue of the Dead and move on to your final two destinations, the Pyramid of the Moon and the Pyramid of the Sun, you move beyond your limited human scope and understand your greater place in the universe—your divinity.

Mother Moon

The Pyramid of the Moon invites people of all walks of life to explore the feminine. Although we all have both masculine and feminine energy inside us, most of us lean heavily toward one or the other—sometimes because of domestications that we never question and sometimes because it simply resonates with us. We use these agreements to forge part of our identities. And just because you are endeavoring on this journey to let your false identity go, that doesn't mean you won't use these energies anymore. The difference is that now you will allow them to flow through you freely when you need them, rather than grabbing on to them and holding them tightly.

Consider what female energy means for you and for your life. What about male energy? Remember: You do not have to adhere to or align with anyone else's definitions of feminine and masculine, which are, after all, based on agreements. When you consider symbols of feminine energy, you can be inspired by icons as diverse as the Virgin Mary or the Hindu goddess Kali. You can be inspired by women *and* by men in your own life, by ancestors, by cultural figures, or even by feminine aspects of nature in animals, plants, and geography.

My grandmother has long been a matriarchal force in my life, as well as having a profound influence on my family's work. She was both a shaman and a *curandera*, or faith healer. She taught in a small spiritual temple called Nueva Vida, in Barrio Logan in San Diego. Every Sunday, she performed what she called a *cátedra*, a spiritual teaching similar to a Mass. Through prayer, she entered into a trance and the Spirit spoke through her. She went on an inner astral journey that allowed her to practice her faith. During the week, she performed healings and consultations there. She was the first woman to be paid by the State of California to be a faith healer for Casa Familiar, a community outreach center in San Ysidro, California in the 1970s. Years later, she was inducted into the San Diego Women's Hall of Fame for her work in the community and her achievements in keeping the family's spiritual tradition alive.

My grandmother's feminine power is still central to my family's teachings today. But even in my home and family, there remain some strong agreements about gender roles. For example, my wife and I have committed to maintaining our home together. When she cooks, I wash dishes, and vice versa. I wash clothes too. When my mother first saw this dynamic, she got very upset. In her upbringing, these were jobs for women. First, she got mad at me because I was doing the "wrong" thing as a man. Then she got mad at my wife for not "taking care" of me. I love my mom and respect her very much, but if I let her dictate what kind of man should be, I would be going back to square one. I unlearned a lot of what my parents domesticated me with. The agreements that were true for them and their love are still true for them today. However, my wife and I do what is true for us. We have created a new culture for ourselves, and our family, with our love and agreements. I am sure that my kids will create their own in their time.

All this is to say that we must be careful of domestications about what it means to be male and female. We all carry these assumptions and distortions within us, and that's perfectly fine. I only ask that you continue to practice awareness, to expose existing agreements and distortions of these ideas that have been the foundation of your conditional love, and find out what you want to do and how you want to express your love.

I like to think of feminine and masculine power in terms of actions rather than descriptions. So, instead of saying someone is sweet or caring, I notice what they are really doing when they are drawing on feminine power.

Maybe they are comforting, healing, or listening. Maybe they are protecting like the modern term of "mama bear," or maybe they are intuiting and confronting a hidden problem that no one else sees. This allows me to think about actively bringing feminine power into my own work and life. In this way, I keep the male and female energies within me in a balanced state, free of any identity-building.

Energetic Doubles

Modern science has discovered that the body renews all of its cells every seven years. So, in a sense, there is literally no part of your tonal that is the same as it was seven years ago. In a more symbolic sense, you can use this idea of multiple selves as a tool for making changes in your life and for healing. Have you ever thought of yourself as more than one person? Or understood that you have an "old self" who is in fact totally different from the current you?

As we lead groups through Teo, when we arrive at the Pyramid of the Moon, we encourage people to visualize their energetic doubles in their own minds to give them a little outside perspective on this other version of themselves. After climbing to the top of the pyramid, they rest of the flat surface alongside their doubles. Then we form a circle at the top of the pyramid and together imagine that our doubles leap into and through the center of the pyramid, taking all our past agreements with them and releasing us into a new life. This is our rebirth.

The Power of Intent

At the top of the Pyramid of the Moon, you also experience the freedom of your own *intent*, a word that has special meaning in the Toltec tradition. Imagine for a moment that you are an eagle, flying high above a pristine valley. You feel the clarity of the element of air all around you as you look down on a vast landscape below. You understand for the first time, through your own incredible wisdom, that the things you once thought were holding you back—thoughts, stories, emotions—don't control you anymore. You have the power to see through them, to find their origins, to rewrite them, to feel them flow, and to let them go. Your psychological fears no longer control you. This is the liberation you feel at the top of the Pyramid of the Moon. This is the new life you have claimed through your arduous journey and your intent.

From here, and from now on, you will consciously practice your intent. Now, at the beginning of your new life, *you* choose where to put your nagual energy. *You* choose how to bring your own singular, passionate spirit out into the world, unencumbered by past agreements and beliefs, and you will create your work of art with impeccable intent. *You* get to express yourself, to love and accept yourself, and to live into the realization that everything you are experiencing actually comes from you, from your own intent. When you realize that intent is the same as unconditional love, there is no limit to the spiraling heights you can create, enjoy, and explore.

EXERCISE: DAYLONG REFLECTION RETREAT

You have done a lot of personal work. You have explored many different deep parts of your inner being. This exercise can help you take your first steps out into the world to see with new eyes and a new sense of freedom. This is a monumental and profound step, so it's fitting to spend some time in reflection and rest in order to absorb the lessons you've learned and prepare yourself to step out over the threshold of personal transformation.

While this exercise is offered in the form of a daylong retreat, you can set aside just a couple of hours for it if your schedule simply won't allow a full day. Try to make the retreat as long as possible, however, as this will enhance its benefits.

For the duration of your retreat, commit to turning off your TV, your cell phone, your laptop, and any other electronic devices you may use. Spend some time beforehand tidying the space you plan to use so you can focus on relaxing and enjoying the space. This is sacred time with your self.

Here are some suggestions for practicing awareness during your retreat:

Cook yourself a meal. Slow down and appreciate each ingredient. Notice how it smells by itself (thyme) in contrast to how it smells in combination with other ingredients (thyme added to cooking onions). Feel the texture of each vegetable; note its color. Try to focus solely on what you are doing in the moment without thinking of other things.

Be grateful. When you sit down to eat, take a few moments to center yourself. Take a few breaths and allow yourself some gratitude for the food in front of you, for the time you took to prepare it, for the people who grew it, etc.

Treat yourself. Choose a favorite food or dessert and eat it very slowly, savoring each bite. This is not some kind of strict "health-conscious" retreat. This is about fully enjoying the physical body you've been given.

Meditate. Sit in meditation, perhaps one of the meditations or visualizations given in this book. Notice if you feel differently now that you are nearing the completion of your journey.

Go outside. Go for a long walk in a natural area. Stop occasionally to stand still and simply notice the world around you—the way the wind is blowing, the feeling of cool or hot air on your skin, the gravel beneath your feet, the sound of birds or airplanes or other people nearby. Try not to judge any of these sensations as better or worse than another. Just feel, see, smell, or hear them.

Take a nap. If you feel tired in the middle of the day, listen to your body and take a nap. Consider turning on some soothing music or opening the window and letting in some fresh air while you doze. Good scents, like food cooking or incense burning, can be helpful too. A friend of mine says that some of her best naps have been while others are cooking, and that the smell of good food simmering on the stove helps her drift off into a delicious dreamy sleep.

Take a bath. Take a long relaxing soak in the tub. Add essential oils or bath salts to your taste.

Exercise. If you practice yoga or qigong, this is a perfect time for these practices.

EXERCISE: SAYING GOODBYE

In this exercise, you build a living image of yourself, a vessel to hold the old agreements and beliefs that made up your prior self, and then send that vessel up and out into the universe.

At Teotihuacan, we create our energetic doubles at the Pyramid of the Moon and walk with them all the way to the top of the pyramid, where we say goodbye and let them go. But you can do this yourself at home as well. Your journal can be very helpful in this process, as it now serves as a written chronicle of your old self. You can use your journal, along with the visualization ceremony offered here, to say goodbye to the old version of you and make way for the new.

First, find some uninterrupted time that you can spend in a private space. The space you use for your regular meditation can work just fine. Next, prepare your space for the ceremony by adding an element to it that evokes the spirit and majesty of the moon. This can be a crystal or an image of the moon. Alternatively, you can find a quiet place outside to perform this ceremony under the light of the moon. Set aside at least thirty minutes to an hour, so you can move completely through the full ceremony.

Once you have created your sacred space, begin by reviewing your journal. Look at the lists you made at the end of chapters 2 and 3. Review your work in the Plaza of the Mind and the plazas of the four elements. This is the story of the old you. Go through these insights one by one. Remember: Your journal is an account of all the ways in which you have created an identity. In a sense, this is your energetic double.

Once you have reviewed your journal, close it and set it aside. Settle into a position that is comfortable for you, either sitting or lying down, and close your eyes. Take several deep, calming breaths and focus your attention on the present moment.

When you feel relaxed, imagine a seed of light in the middle of your chest, just below your heart (at your solar plexus). On every inhalation, imagine the light of the nagual entering your body, growing brighter and brighter as it does so. See the light filling your torso, your arms and hands and fingers, your legs, feet, and toes, traveling up into your throat and your head. On every breath, this light grows brighter, filling every cell of your being. Once you have taken a few deep breaths and the light of the nagual fills your body, imagine this light duplicating itself and stepping outside of you. This light now assumes the shape of your body and turns to face you. Picture the light fading to a radiant, but less intense, glow than your own light, and imagine you can see your features just beneath the light of this double. Take a moment to send a wave of gratitude to this other you.

Hold that image in front of you and consider again all the domestications, agreements, and beliefs you are ready to let go. See them leaving you and entering your double.

Next, imagine taking the hand of your energetic double and, together, turning to face the symbol of the moon in your sacred space, or the actual moon if you are outside. Imagine you are standing together on the top of a great pyramid at night, with the whole of the dark earth laid out below you as far as you can see. Look at the astonishing vault of the starry sky above you. Everything everywhere is lit up with the luminous, silvery light of the moon, which shines directly overhead.

When you are ready, release the hand of your energetic double and watch as it moves silently and joyfully up into the sky, taking with it all vestiges of your old self—the agreements and beliefs you no longer need and are now releasing into the universe to be recycled back into pure nagual. Imagine as you do so that you feel lighter, refreshed, free, and filled with a silvery radiant newness. This is your rebirth. This is the beginning of your new life, free and utterly transformed, filled with unconditional love and the artistry of a life lived in accordance with its ultimate purpose.

Once you feel this process is complete, come back to your awareness of your tonal, your physical body, standing in front of your representation of the moon. Feel your feet planted on the ground. Move your arms slowly and stretch a bit. When you are ready, open your eyes and look around. The world may not have changed, but you have.

Next, I invite you to discard your journal. Doing so is a symbol of saying goodbye to the old you. If you are not ready to part with it yet, that's okay too. For instance, perhaps there is still some forgiveness work you need to do in which your journal may be of help. You will know when it's time to discard it.

Chapter 10

The Pyramid of the Sun

In 1609, Galileo Galilei aimed a self-made spyglass at the skies above his home, making a series of observations that would turn the conventional understanding of his time on its head. His curious exploration proved that the earth was not, in fact, the center of our solar system. Rather it revolved around the sun along with the rest of the planets. Of course, Galileo's great and redefining gift of scientific truth was met with fear and scorn, and he was placed under house arrest for the final ten years of his life. But the truth could not be dimmed. Galileo had witnessed and measured the light of the sun and its reflection onto the planets as they circled. His transformative understanding burned away the illusion of an unmoving earth and paved the way for centuries of deeper knowledge.

When you begin the journey of the mastery of life, you are like Galileo. You start in one place, believing whatever you believe. You have no other choice, and this is not a bad thing. And then your curiosity pushes you toward some new information, a little more awareness. You transform. You may even frighten yourself with your discoveries, especially if they run counter to the collective wisdom of your family and friends. You may also frighten others with your willingness to tell the truth of what you see and know. You may try to shut it all down, to run back to your Island of Safety, to the comfort of your past identity. But the truth cannot be dimmed, in fact it exists whether you believe it or not. This is the opposite of a belief or an agreement, which cease to exist the very moment you no longer believe nor agree with it. Once you know the truth, you cannot unknow it.

Just as conventional belief once held that the earth was flat and stationary in the middle of our solar system, your own little self spends much of its early life trying to conform to a version of reality that puts it at the center of everything. Now that you have arrived at the massive Pyramid of the Sun, however, you can shine a light that will burn away this illusion once and for all. As you move toward the close of your journey, you can maintain compassion and forgive yourself for any past judgments, for the identities you accepted, and the ways you hurt yourself and others. You are ready step into the life-giving warmth and light of the sun and create a whole new dream.

Standing in the Light

The Pyramid of the Sun is the largest of all the structures at Teotihuacan. Indeed, it is among the largest ancient pyramids in the Western Hemisphere. At the tip of this colossal structure is where the sun and the earth make love to create life.

Leading up from the pyramid's base is a long line of steps that reaches up toward the sky, as if you could climb up them to the sun itself. Two sets of steps at the bottom come together in a single wide staircase in the middle, and then diverge again into two parallel and more narrow sets of steps. When you make your way to the top of the pyramid and look back on where you have come, you see the pattern of the stairs behind you. The paths form the shape of a person with raised arms, as if the sun's brightness casts a massive shadow of a person down the side of the pyramid. This is the modern facade of the pyramid, which has been in place since a restoration project at the beginning of the twentieth century that was led by archaeologist Leopoldo Batres and commisioned by General Porfirio Díaz.

In my family's tradition, we see this final passage as a beautiful metaphor for what happens here spiritually. This is the place where you reawaken your divinity, where you ascend into infinity. This shadow indicates the way you must follow, step-by-step, to the summit of the pyramid.

To my knowledge, there is no native culture on earth that does not respect and honor the sun. In many ancient cultures, the sun was often understood to be a god, or even the ruler of all the gods. And it's no wonder, since we now know through science that the sun is what gives life to all matter in our solar system. Without it, nothing we know as life would exist. That is why the sun—and the light and heat it emits—is the most powerful physical and symbolic representation of the nagual available to us.

Father Sun

The sun also represents the masculine energy within us, and we can call on that energy whenever we need or want to. But, just as with the feminine energy of the moon, we have to be aware of the temptation to fall into domestications about it. We don't get to choose or dictate how this energy moves through us into the world; we don't need to say whether it is "good" or "bad."

Just as we all have feminine energy within us, everyone carries masculine energy as well. Some of my associations are the male aspects of playing and competition. There are also other aspects: Adventuring, leaping without a net. Speaking plainly and openly. Building with care and effort. Self-focusing on improvement and goals. Protecting and setting boundaries. I assign a masculine energy to all of these, although they may be totally different for you. But above all else, it is about creating and holding space for life to blossom.

In recent years, when my father has climbed the Pyramid of the Sun during our journeys at Teo, he has found that he can no longer do it in the way he could when he was younger, especially after his massive heart attack. On a recent trip, he had to take three steps and sit down, then another three steps and sit down, until he reached the top. He rested and listened to his body, got himself out of the way and just let intent flow through him, letting it tell him when he was ready for his next few steps. Rather than becoming aggravated or upset, he was able to embrace the truth for him in that moment—that he should not wish for things to be different than they were; that he should not yearn for a return to the past; that he should not fear a future that was yet to come, just be pure life in action in the here and now.

His faith in life manifested through the voice of "the ally," a mind that was redeemed and healed by letting go of the domestication that distorted it and becomes an instrument by which one can create with awareness. And watching him let go, I could also accept the truth. I saw in my father's actions a teaching for my own life. In that moment, I learned to stop worrying about what could be and instead engage with what was present in order to create my own work of art based on this truth. This is freedom. Faith is setting your intent in something without a doubt, such as truth in action. I am alive at this moment, and while there is life, anything is possible. This is the sun shining its light, burning away the illusion of past and future.

Your Unique Light

Your existence in the universe is like a unique ray of light from the sun. Like snowflakes, sunbeams come in infinite variations, and no two will ever be the same. Much of the domestication you receive is an attempt to convince you that you have to change your ray of light or disguise it so that it looks like all the others, to assimilate to someone else's dream. Now, having traversed the Avenue of the Dead and released the final remnants of your domesticated past into the Pyramid of the Moon, you are ready to embody the unique sunbeam that is you.

Just as a sunbeam emanates from the sun itself, your life comes *from* the nagual and you *are* the nagual. You are the energy that animates life itself. Nothing more, nothing less. Now that you know that—not only in your mind, but in your experience as well—you can claim your new life and reconnect with the nagual inside you. Your domesticated past may present itself from time to time in emotional reactions or old habits, but these, along with your past traumas and beliefs, no longer control you. You have let them go and embraced personal freedom.

In the Toltec tradition, we say that, just as the sunbeam carries its message from the sun, you are a messenger and your life becomes your message. Don't confuse this with trying to convert others and push your message on them, however. We don't do that. We don't believe in spreading any one doctrine or attempting to control any other person's life or journey. Rather, we endeavor to have our actions flow from the deep well of the unconditional love that animates the universe. The whole point of this journey has been to cleanse the path for this love to flow through you. Your actions now speak volumes as you choose the life you want to live and decide how you will fashion the message of your life, without a doubt.

Because we don't proselytize, some take this to mean that helping others is not a component of the Toltec path.

But nothing could be farther from the truth. We understand that there is no real "help" in telling others what to do. In the current Dream of the Planet, that is a trap of domestication, not an offer of freedom. We help others by allowing our actions to be mirrors for them on their own spiritual journeys and by lending our personal power in support of those who are treading the difficult path of the Toltec Warrior. In this way, we live in service to others by being in service to life itself.

When Toltec Warriors teach, talk, and even write, all of these are secondary practices to helping others. The primary goal of how we live our own lives is to do what has the potential to be the most helpful. I have watched this particular dynamic unfold several times between my father and a new apprentice. Some who come to our workshops or retreats are very eager to please. They want to validate their experiences, to know that what they are doing is worthwhile and important.

Sometimes the way they approach this is to be "good students" in the presence of the "Nagual," and in this stage of their journey they only understand a Nagual to be a spiritual teacher or guide. There is nothing good or bad about this, of course, but my father recognizes it right away when people try to gather his attention and energy to support the goals of their "little selves" that their

Island of Safety has shaped. And yet he never mentions this to anyone. He does not point out their behavior or talk about it. He simply ignores the masks that they have chosen to wear or are wearing out of habit. This form of unconditional love from my father may feel like rejection at first. But it's simply an action based in a choice not to give any power to the behavior. And through his actions, my father's lessons become clear very quickly. If you are working to release the identity of the little self, he will support you and share his love by paying no attention to this little self's masks.

Teaching Without Words

While words coming from the right intent can certainly be helpful to others, they are secondary tools that are only truly helpful when matched with our actions. For instance, you are likely familiar with the old parental directive to "do as I say and not as I do." But this demand is rarely, if ever, effective. We are always teaching our young ones, and everyone else with whom we come in contact, through our actions.

When my children were little, my wife had a habit of cleaning up after them and at the same time complaining about how they never cleaned up after themselves. At a certain point, she realized that her words and her actions were at cross-purposes. She could still use words, but she had to aim them differently. She started to experiment to see what would work. Once, when she encountered a toy in the hallway and the children were nearby, she staged an over-the-top, silly, dramatic fall. Her ridiculous panto-mime made the children start laughing. Then, they put *all* their toys in the hall so that everyone in the house could pretend to fall down over and over, yelping and crying and getting "hurt." At the end of this game, it was obvi-ously time to clean up together, and so we did. Strangely enough, the children got the message about the toys in the hallway, and they put them away.

Sometimes to be a teacher, you don't have to speak at all.

I have a friend who told me about a woman in his twelve-step recovery group for alcoholism. For several years before this woman joined the group, she lived in a neighborhood where there was a well-known "neighbor-hood drunk." The man in question lived alone. There were mountains of alcohol bottles in his trash each week. The grass and plants in his yard grew wild and scraggly; there were broken window shades in the filthy windows; and his dinged-up car was always pulled into the driveway at a strange angle. Everybody knew this guy had a prob-lem with alcohol. No one had to say it.

Then, one day, the woman noticed that the lawn was mowed, the car was straight in the driveway, the windows were clean, and the shades were fixed. On trash day, there were no more empty alcohol containers stuffed into overflowing trash cans. Day by day, week by week, everything about the look of the house and its energy got better. This continued for several years. Then the man died. The woman never met him.

But as he was fixing up his home and cleaning up his act, this woman had been spiraling downward into her own cycle of drinking and addiction. When she finally bottomed out, she asked a neighbor what the old nieghborhood drunk had done to get his life back on track. The neighbor's answer was simple: He went to AA. It was so obvious. She had witnessed the transformation herself. So the woman turned to AA, where she was helped, and she was led there by a person to whom she never spoke and whom she never even met. She has now been sober for ten years.

The old man in the run-down house had served as a messenger with just his actions. He never knew how far his message reached and the profound effect it had on this woman's life and, by extension, on all of the people whose lives she touched.

Your Life Is the Message

We don't have to talk about the profound teachings we have inside us. In fact, in many cases it's better that we don't. At the beginning of this book, I suggested that you let my words go around your mind and into your heart, yet many people may not be able to do this. In those cases, my words may even become an obstacle, because their minds will hear me and immediately put up a wall. For these people, it is better to be silent and let actions speak instead.

In the end, our actions are the most important message we share. And we pass on this message by remembering that we are the artists who create our own masterpieces through how we live. When you live as a Toltec Warrior, you know that, in the mastery of life, you are the messenger and your life is the message. You were domesticated once, but now you have a choice.

In fact, the entire Toltec way is about choice. We honor the autonomy of each person's personal power and respect their choices to do what is true for them, and we respect them to experience the consequences of those choices. A consequence is not a punishment, as some might associate it with during their domestication, but rather it is the result of a choice or action taken. In our view, reality itself is knowable only from the individual perspective, the personal dream. And we acknowledge that the only one you can change is yourself. This may sound selfish to some, but in knowing this truth and embracing it in the bright sun of unconditional love, you shed your old identity and allow the unbounded self, the nagual, to emerge and play through you.

In this way, changing your own perspective becomes an orientation—a place to begin—not a prison or an obsession. Once the parasite transforms into your ally and you become the artist of your life, you love and respect all of creation. Here at the Pyramid of the Sun, you step into your life as an artist, consciously cocreating the Dream of the Planet with every other living thing, yet knowing you are only responsible for your own perception.

What does this creative artistry look like? For some, it means writing music, choreographing dances, or creating other works of art. It may also mean working with nature, exploring science, or creating new technologies. For others, it may be the work of raising children, maintaining a home, or guiding others on their own personal journeys. For most, it will be a combination of several things. But through it all, the most powerful gift you can offer yourself and others is to extend your unconditional love in all situations, especially when that self-love feels shaky as a result of the voices of the mitote.

Remember: No one does this perfectly. The mastery of life is about learning to recognize when fear has crept in and making the choice to return to love. This inner work sometimes dovetails with powerful activism for certain causes. As Dr. Martin Luther King Jr. taught: "Only through an inner spiritual transformation do we gain the strength to fight vigorously the evils of the world in a humble and loving spirit."

Whatever you choose to do, your sunbeam will play and dream in its own way. It's up to you. It's your creation, your work of art. Now, go and conquer death by becoming alive.

Conclusion

Journey's End

And so we find ourselves on the final peak of the last pyramid of our symbolic journey through Teotihuacan.

You can read a book, take a workshop, or travel to a sacred place. And all of that can support you, but it is not the same as doing the work itself. The real work is not what you learn from this book, or in a classroom, or on top of a pyramid. The real work starts when you live your life and apply the teachings. You will not see the impact of your journey from inside your own head. You will only see it through trying, failing, learning, and trying again.

What I hope I have given you in the pages of this book is the same thing that I hope to impart to apprentices that go through the sacred ceremonies at Teo. In this space, you give yourself permission to make a new choice, like the permission to heal from an old wound, for example. You arrive at the choice that now shines brilliantly before you, like a sun. You can continue to believe your old illusion, or you can work to change your life into something else. This work will take place, not in the holy temples and plazas of Teo, but rather in the sacred spaces you interact with every day—your body, your mind, your home, your heart, your relationships, your family, your work, and your joys.

You have given yourself permission to make this choice. Either way, it's up to you.

My purpose in telling you these stories—giving you these perspectives from my own life, these reflections that come from inside me—is to share with you that *it can be done*, that change is possible, that fear does not need to control you, and that you can create your own masterpiece of a life. When you bring the journey into your own life—when you use these lessons to heal yourself—it can only come from you.

I often describe a personal journey as similar to the journey of becoming a parent. New mothers and fathers get bombarded with rules, advice, and information about what to do and what not to do with their children. But this information is often conflicting and overwhelming, and often has little bearing on their actual circumstances.

But as time progresses, they start to have trust in themselves. They know what works and what doesn't. They learn what advice was terrible for them and their child, even if it may have worked well for somebody else. Spirituality, and indeed any form of self-work, operates in the same way. You don't know until you do it.

At the end of this journey, you may realize that you want to make some profound changes in your life. Or you may not. Your life may not look outwardly different to anyone else. You don't have to change careers, set aside friendships, or end your relationships. You may still do all the things you did before. And yet, through the mastery of life, you are totally different. You are no longer trapped in endless cycles of psychological fear. You are no longer bound to this world or any one identity within it. You are an artist of your own life—creating, experiencing, and reflecting the beauty of life itself.

The mastery of life is a journey of transformation, not transcendence. You are not going to exist in a higher spiritual frequency, floating above others in superior awareness or grace. That is a story manufactured by the ego. The journey is one of unlearning. When you unlearn your previous patterns, you realize that the nagual inside you, your unique ray of sunlight, did not need any improvement. It did not need to grow. The nagual is always right here, right now, ready to connect with you, to remind you that you are perfect right now in the present moment. You can dream and play; you can flow. You can accept and give unconditional love. You can offer your life in service to life itself.

So what are you going to do?

Acknowledgments

I want to honor my family, the source of love, joy, and compassion in my life. Thank you for every moment we have spent sharing and enjoying life together. I love you all very much!

I want to honor and thank Randy Davila, my publisher/editor/ink-brother, and his team at Hierophant Publishing. Thank you for the opportunity to continue to share my family's traditon through this whole body of work. I am humbled by what we have created together and what is to come. Thank you, Carnal! Love you!

I want to honor and thank my dear friend, Kristie Macris, who helped me find my voice and guided me through the mitote of my first drafts. You are my teacher. ¡Te amo!

I want to honor and thank you ink-sister, Heather-Ash Amara. High Five! I am so glad that we will continue to cocreate for many years to come. Love you!

I want to honor my apprentices, who gave me the space and time to share these teachings with you. To Kirk, Misty, Greg, Lily, Vanessa, Tara, Paul, Mark, Jess, Roxanne, and Leslie and in loving memory of Heather Lorah, big hugs with all of my love!

To my teachers, don Miguel Ruiz, don José Ruiz, and Madre Sarita. Los quiero!

Gracias a Dios.

About the Author

Don Miguel Ruiz Jr. is a Nagual, a Toltec Master of Transformation. He is a direct descendant of the Toltecs of the Eagle Knight lineage and the son of don Miguel Ruiz. By combining the wisdom of his family's traditions with the knowledge gained from his own personal journey, he now helps others realize their own path to personal freedom. His bestselling titles include *The Mastery of Self, The Five Levels of Attachment,* and *Living a Life of Awareness.* Visit him at *www.miguelruizjr.com.*

Also from Hierophant Publishing

Available wherever books are sold.